MR PRESIDENT?

*BE CAREFUL WHO YOU VOTE
FOR!*

CHRIS WHALEY AND
MIKE MCCLASKEY

PUBLISHING

Mr President ? Be Careful Who You Vote For !
Copyright © 2023 by Chris Whaley and Mike McClaskey

For information contact :
ATG Publishing
info@atgpublishing.com - http://www.atgpublishing.com

ISBN: 9781991123220

First Edition: November 2023

10 9 8 7 6 5 4 3 2 1

Dedication

"I've often said if I lost everything I own and still had my girls, I would still be a very rich man. I dedicate this book to my three girls. My wife of 48 years, Verna. My oldest daughter and mother of my four oldest grandkids, Alyson. My youngest and mother of my two youngest grandkids, Kacie. I'm a blessed man."

Chris Whaley

"I'd be remiss in giving thanks if I didn't mention my family, starting with Jackie, for all their support and love over the years. However, if I'm going to acknowledge someone, that would be my father, AC McClaskey. In my 65 years I've never known anyone so willing to give of themselves. Financially, spiritually, and morally. Everything I have, do, or dream of doing is because of the sacrifices he made. I know he would enjoy this book and I hope you do also. Enjoy."

Mike McClaskey

Chapter One

The Making of a Comedian

It was a story that started like a million other stories. It was a no-name poor family in a small town in Iowa in January 1961. Part of the story centres on the only son of a single mom, but the outcome of this life made quite an impact years later. That may happen in other similar settings, but not like this one. This one was special. It's amazing what God can do to fix lives that look broken.

Redding, Iowa, was a city of about ten thousand. Just like the majority of small towns, there were those undereducated, underprivileged people who lived on the proverbial "other side" of the tracks. Blanche Conners and six-year-old Timmy comfortably fit into that group. They lived in a dilapidated housing section overrun with trash and waste, where the local drunks slept off their welfare check boxed wine. The Conners lived in a small one-bedroom cracker box, roach-infested apartment that smelled about as bad as it looked to the eye.

Timmy was either twenty pounds overweight or a foot too short for his weight. The food-stained Goodwill T-shirt he wore was about two sizes too small. His hand-me-down sweatpants were about two sizes too big. His socks had holes in them, and a brush hadn't touched his hair or his teeth in a long time. Timmy was a fun-loving boy who had no idea his home life left a lot to be desired. In his mind he was a normal kid, in a normal family.

On Saturday mornings he usually watched cartoons on a nineteen-inch black-and-white Zenith with rabbit ears, and tinfoil carefully applied to the antenna to enhance reception.

The Conners' furniture consisted of a couch rescued from a dumpster, some upside-down milk crates served as tables, and bedsheet curtains which masked cracked windows. Nothing matched and everything bore a cigarette-smoke film, from the little television screen to the refrigerator.

While Timmy was tuning in his favorite cartoons, the sound of the toilet flushing broke his concentration. His mom walked out of the bathroom and scratched herself in an unladylike manner. The sound of the Timmy's cartoons crashed into Blanche's skull like waves thrashing the rocks along the Northern California coast. A hangover maximized the sound emanating from the television.

"Turn that stupid TV down! The whole building can hear what you're watching!"

Blanche made her way to a wobbly card table. Even though she was in her thirties, she looked older. She had shopping bags under her eyes, more wrinkles than a California prune, and a thick, raspy, croaky voice. Blanche was not only a smoker but also a heavy drinker. It was easy to see why she never remarried but hard to understand how anyone could deem her fit to raise a child.

She lit a cigarette even though one was still burning in an ashtray. When she saw Timmy head toward the bathroom, she called out, "I wouldn't go in there right now. Those tacos taste great when you're eating them, but they leave a terrible fog the next morning."

Timmy turned back to his cartoon-watching while holding his nose with two fingers.

His breakfast was on the table. Blanche, as usual, knocked herself out fixing it for him. A bowl of no-name cereal, a can of soda—both from a nearby dollar store—and some day-old donuts from the dumpster behind the bakery. Blanche drank her breakfast when Timmy wasn't looking.

Timmy changed the channel to another show but

stopped when he detected a news show voice. The president of the United States was making a speech. Timmy stared at President Kennedy and heard him say, "Ask not what your country can do for you—ask what you can do for your country." The six-year-old seemed mesmerized by the words.

"Hey, Mom," he called out. "Can I be president someday?"

Blanche sat in a stupor at the table, oblivious to what Timmy had chanced upon.

"What?" she mumbled, somewhat annoyed.

"Can I be president someday?" Timmy repeated, pointing at Kennedy.

His mom leaned toward the television to see what he was talking about, and watched a few minutes of the inaugural address. Suddenly she burst out laughing.

"Ha, you're too funny! You...President? That's a good one. You're a real comedian. That's what you ought to be. A comedian!"

Timmy shrugged his shoulders as if to agree with her. He turned the knob to the next channel and hit pay dirt: The Bugs Bunny Roadrunner Show.

Chapter Two

The Making of a World Champion

San Diego is beautiful year-round; the weather is gorgeous, the land is beautiful, and the city is one of the greatest in America. It was 1984, inside a nice apartment complex on a Saturday morning. The other part of the story centers around six-year-old Anthony "Butch" Vernon. He's an all-American kid. Butch was sitting on a spacious couch in a well-decorated living room, using the large-screen television's remote to find something to watch.

Butch was a great-looking African American kid wearing He-Man pajamas, cradling a stuffed wrestling figure in one hand and the remote in the other.

His mother, Sydney, sat at an oversized, handcrafted dining room table, paying her bills. Even though it was morning, and she was still in her pajamas, she looked fabulous. Not a hair out of place, manicured nails, and no makeup (she didn't need it). She would take a bite of her breakfast in between stuffing envelopes with checks and payment stubs.

On the table, across from her, was Butch's breakfast of scrambled eggs, whole wheat toast, fruit, and orange juice, with a Flintstone vitamin waiting next to the juice glass. So far Butch hadn't touched his breakfast because he was searching for something to watch. Sydney didn't seem to mind his distraction.

Butch paused on a channel because of a voice. President Ronald Reagan was in the midst of a speech. Butch dropped the remote and walked closer to the TV, soaking in the president's words.

A moment later he turned to his mom, pointed at the TV and said, "Hey, Mom, can I be president someday?"

Sydney, not sure what Butch was talking about, leaned over to see what he was pointing at and watched for a moment.

"What did you say, baby?"

Butch repeated, "When I grow up, can I be president?"

Sydney smiled and said, "You can be anything you want to be when you grow up! But you need to do well in school, work hard, and follow God's will for your life. You're a smart young man. If you want to be president, you can be president!" Then she went back to her checkbook.

Butch returned to channel surfing and stopped on a WWF Wrestling Saturday morning cable show. As he watched, he began doing wrestling holds on his wrestling doll and jumped up on the couch and then off, tumbling to the floor. When he stood up, he raised his hands as if he were the champion.

"If I can be anything I want to be when I grow up, I want to be the world heavyweight wrestling champion!"

Butch's eyes were fixed on Hulk Hogan as he marched to the ring in his gold muscle shirt, gold tights, and gold boots. He pointed at his opponent in the ring and pointed to the crowd and then held his hand to his ear to encourage the crowd to cheer for him. He entered the ring, tore his muscle shirt in half, and threw it to a fan in the crowd. Butch was excited as he watched his hero.

After another victorious win in the match, Hulk talked to Mean Gene about an upcoming match with Rowdy Roddy Piper. After sharing what he planned to do with his opponent, he stared into the camera and said, "To all my little Hulkamaniacs out there, if you want to be a champion like me, you need to say your prayers, eat your vitamins, and train hard!"

Butch dropped the wrestling doll and ran over to the table. He ate his eggs and toast and washed down his vitamins with a big gulp of orange juice. Then he ran back into the living room and made several attempts at doing push-ups in front of the TV.

Sydney was captivated by her little man's routine. She smiled, shook her head, and finished paying the bills.

Chapter Three

The Beginning of a Scam Artist

Our story moves back to 1968 and picks up with Timmy. He is now in the sixth grade at Longleaf Middle School. He's not the greatest student, but far from stupid. Growing up where he did, he learned to survive by using his wits. To the surprise of some, he demonstrates strong leadership skills and has a small following of classmates from the same background.

Timmy is thirteen years old and still twenty pounds overweight. He doesn't look menacing in his jeans and thrift-store shirt and tennis shoes, but it's obvious who's in charge among the other boys in his class.

He and a few friends are in a restroom with large stalls next to the gym. He had swiped a few of his mom's cigarettes to find out why she seemed to enjoy smoking so much. He first experimented with a few of her leftover butts, but this was the first time he had a single untouched cigarette.

Timmy had planned everything out in his mind as to how this experiment would go. Peewee would act as the lookout, holding the door open just enough to see if anyone was coming down the hallway. The others could almost hear his heart pounding as Peewee anxiously performed his duty.

Timmy stood under a window that was cracked just enough to allow the smoke to escape once the cigarette was lit. As he looked at the cigarette and at his fellow cohorts, he thought he might enlarge his persona even more by mentioning he had his eye on one of the campus beauties.

"That Missy is sure turning into a fine-looking woman, isn't she? I've noticed her shirt fits differently this year than it did last year, if you know what I mean!" he said with some swagger in his voice.

The boys were puzzled and looked at each other. "Of course, her shirt fits different than last year. We're getting older and putting on weight!" said Howie, who was not much bigger than Peewee.

"Are you really that stupid, Howie? Oh, forget it. Let's get this party started!" Timmy said with a hint of disdain in his voice.

Peewee turned his attention back to the hallway and

saw someone coming. It was Mr. Haskell, the dean of students. Jackson Haskell was in his fifties, wearing knit slacks, a striped dress shirt, and a wide orange tie. His comb-over and straggly mustache made him the brunt of a lot of jokes among the students, but he wasn't a joke when it came to discipline.

"Cheese it! Here comes Dean Haskell!" yelled the lookout in a high-pitched voice.

Peewee, Howie, and the other boys ran straight toward the window. They jumped up on the metal sink and pulled themselves through the open window to safety and never looked back.

Timmy ran over, threw the cigarette into the closest toilet and gave it a flush. He then headed toward the window, but it was a struggle for him to get up on the sink. Unlike his buddies, the pudgy punster became stuck in the window, with his feet flailing in midair.

Dean Haskell entered the restroom and saw Timmy's feet frantically thrashing the air. With his hands on his hips, he shook his head. He knew who was stuck in the window. A moment later he grabbed Timmy's feet and belt and pulled him down.

"Follow me to my office, young man! And don't get lost on the way. As a matter of fact, you walk ahead of me so we can make sure you make it," Haskell said with a booming voice.

As they walked to the dean's office, the bell rang, and the hallways were flooded with students. Most of them gawked at the obvious capture. Timmy's small band of friends came through a door beyond the side of the gym in time to see their leader in Dean Haskell's custody.

Timmy and the dean entered the latter's office, and Haskell pointed to the chair in front of the desk. While Timmy took a seat, the dean opened a file cabinet drawer and fished out a thick folder. He threw it on his desk and sat down. Haskell leafed through the two-inch-thick stack of papers.

"Wow, Conners, you're a real piece of work. Your behavior has been chronicled like a crime sheet," he said without looking up. "You know, I would call your mom, but I'm not sure which bar to call to reach her. So why don't we just handle this in house."

The dean's eyes lifted from the folder on his desk to a large paddle hanging on the wall, and then he slowly looked at Timmy. The paddle was engraved "Attitude Adjustment" in large letters.

"I believe you've gone before the board previously, haven't you? This shouldn't be a big deal for you. You need to stand, empty your pockets, and bend over." A sinister smile filled his face.

Timmy rolled his eyes, reached into his back pocket and pulled out a wrinkled photo, placing it face down on the desk. He smiled and looked at the photo and then Dean Haskell.

"You're married, right, Dean Haskell?"

The question confused the school administrator for a moment. He cleared his throat and said, "Yes, of course I'm married. What business is that of yours?"

Timmy leaned forward and flipped the picture over, landing it right in front of Dean Haskell. He squinted as he looked at the picture and realized it was a picture of him. He straightened in his chair and looked at Timmy with eyes wide open.

Timmy smiled, leaned back in his chair, and put his feet up on the dean's desk.

"I don't think Mrs. Haskell would be too happy to find out what you and Miss Spivey do after school lets out every day. Sorry about the picture being so grainy. It's hard to get a good shot through that treated glass you guys got here. I have some other pictures that are much clearer than this one, but they're hidden away."

Timmy sat up in the chair. "Wow, Dean, what were you and Miss Spivey doing? That looks like a pretty strange way of keeping your wedding vows."

Dean Haskell dropped the picture to his desk, put his

head in his hands, and groaned.

Timmy put his feet back on the desk and pushed back in his chair. "So, here's how I see this working out Dean Haskell . . ."

Later, Timmy walked out of the dean's office like a conquering king. He swaggered out into the busy hallway and quickly found his fellow felons bunched together. Their faces were filled with fear, which turned into surprise when they saw Timmy approach. He gave them a big smile and a thumbs-up sign.

He said, "Hey, guys, I'm heading to the can for a smoke. Who wants to join me?"

Chapter Four

The Beginning of Greatness!

In 1992, the science fair was kind of a big deal at Cypress Creek Middle School in San Diego. All the kids were excited as they went from exhibit to exhibit, looking at the amazing accomplishments of each student.

Thirteen-year-old Butch Vernon stood near his exhibit. His commitment to fitness was evident even though he had to wear dress slacks, polo, and a sports jacket for the event. On top of everything, he looked sharp. He had done an amazing job of putting together his science project: an active volcano.

The majority of students situated near Butch were girls. It was easy to distinguish the difference between the projects the other students had formulated, and the one Butch had finished. His was a step above. Butch was a stickler for detail, and he did not cut any corners on his project.

Three science teachers and the vice principal were the judges for the science fair. They methodically moved from project to project and recorded their impressions on yellow pads. Every now and then they glanced at each other and smiled, or occasionally rolled their eyes.

When they arrived at Butch's project, they all raised their eyes at the same time. This project stood out compared to the other projects they had judged thus far. Butch was standing to the side with note cards and a handsome smile.

"This is my volcano recreation," he said. "The name volcano comes from the Roman god of fire, Vulcan. Volcanoes occur when there is a crack in the earth's crust, causing molten rock to shoot up to the surface. This molten rock is called magma. Some of the largest volcanoes are found in Hawaii."

Butch put down his note cards, slipped on his safety glasses, and flipped a switch on the back of his display. Smoke slowly rose from the opening of his volcano, then some reddish Jell-O served as magma trickled down the side. It was very impressive.

The judges nodded their heads as they made some notes. A gathering of students, mostly girls, clustered around Butch's project. Some of the girls were more impressed with Butch than the smoldering volcano. He felt a little uncomfortable as he looked away from their googling glares. Some applauded after Butch took off his safety glasses and ended his presentation.

"And that's my report on the volcano. Thank you."

Several students mobbed Butch with congratulatory pats and hugs while the judges made their way to the podium to compare notes and determine the awards. It didn't take them long to agree on a winner.

The principal tapped the microphone at the lectern and announced, "It's time for the award presentations for our science fair. Please gather around!"

There were several awards for various categories, but the grand prize was for the overall winner. Several of the students were called forward to accept their awards. The excitement was extremely high when the principal finally revealed, "And the winner of the Cypress Creek Middle School Science Fair is ... Anthony Vernon!"

Butch smiled as one of the judges placed the medal around his neck. Another judge presented him with a certificate. The principal concluded the award presentation by adding, "As well as receiving the medal and certificate for his outstanding work, Anthony will receive a one-hundred-dollar gift certificate to the San Diego Science Center."

Again, Butch was mobbed by his classmates, and received congratulatory handshakes and hugs from the judges. Butch felt very proud as he stood beside the principal for a photo that would appear in the yearbook.

When the event was over, Butch maneuvered through the crowded hallway to his locker. Various students slapped him on the back and said, "Way to go, Butch!" Several of the girls gave him big smiles and winks. So much attention made Butch feel a little uncomfortable.

Near his locker he saw Tami, standing with an armful of books and notebooks. She made eye contact with Butch and hoped he might help her by holding her books so she could open her locker.

A step or two later Butch saw Patrick, the school bully, knock the books out of Tami's hands. Books and papers flew in several directions onto the floor.

"Sorry, nerd, you're in my way!" the bully said and smirked at her. Patrick received some high fives from some friends.

Butch saw tears forming in Tami's eyes as he knelt to help her pick up her books and papers. After helping her, he said, "Wait here. I'll be right back!"

Butch followed Patrick down the hallway. Tami looked a little confused, but she stayed where she was.

A few minutes later Butch returned with Patrick, and

she saw Butch had Patrick by the arm. Patrick's hair was messed up, his shirt was torn, and there was a reddish welt under one of his eyes. He certainly didn't look as arrogant as he had a few minutes before.

"Do you have something to say to Tami?" Butch said roughly.

Patrick's head was bowed as he said, "Um...I'm... I'm... uh...very sorry for—"

Butch leaned closer to the bully's ear and whispered, "Speak up and say what you've got to say. We're late for class!"

"I'm sorry I knocked your books out of your hands. Please forgive me. I won't do it again!" Patrick said, looking to Butch for his approval.

"Well, thank you for apologizing. I hope you won't do it again," Tami said.

Patrick left in a hurry, and Tami said to Butch, "Thank you so much for your help. That was very brave and kind of you."

Butch said, "No problem, Tami. That guy is a jerk. Someone needed to cut him down to size. Are you all right now?"

"I'm fine now, thanks to you," she said with a smile.

"Well, I hope the rest of your day is much better! We need to get to class," Butch said.

The two smiled at each other as they walked down the hall. Butch was a conquering hero to Tami.

Chapter Five

Comedian for Hire!

Comedy clubs were popular in 1980. Of course, some were upscale, and some were downright disgusting. Timmy worked in the latter. His was a sports bar that doubled as a comedy club. The stage was formed from a collection of pallets with sheets of plywood covering them. There were also a couple of poorly mounted spotlights on the walls, pointed toward the stage.

Timmy was in his early twenties, with thick curly hair, and needing a shave. Those extra twenty pounds were still very prominent on his frame. The bright lights caused him to sweat profusely. His routine needed a lot of work. Timmy had been hired to wait tables, but his boss allowed him to attempt some standup comedy, especially when one of the booked comics didn't show up. Timmy wasn't very good, but the price was right for the boss—free.

"You know why policemen stink?" He paused. "Because they are always on duty." When the punch line elicited only a few titters of laughter, he coached the small crowd, "Get it?" A few more chuckles sounded.

"Say, after the show tonight, maybe a few of us can go by the cemetery and dig up a few dates! I hear the hot chicks are dying to get in there!"

The crowd again had little response, most of the small crowd groaned.

Timmy attempted to look through the lights and the smoke-filled room. The few people there were not paying any attention to him.

His mom, Blanche, was seated at a table in the back, attempting to blend into the wall, out of sight.

Timmy was obviously feeling the heat. He took a dish towel from around his neck and wiped the sweat from his forehead.

"Holy smokes! Is it hot in here or is it just me?"

No one paid him any attention.

"Maybe I can get management to set this up inside the kitchen next week. It might be a little cooler working in front of the deep fryers!"

The only laughter was Timmy's nervous clucks as he continued to mop his sweat.

Blanche leaned toward a nearby table. "That's my boy

up there," she said. Then she picked up her empty glass. "Any of you fine gentlemen want to buy me a drink? My glass is empty." The two men looked at each other and then toward the manager standing to the right of the stage. They made a slashed throat sign, begging him to end the nightmare onstage. The manager went up and took the microphone away from Timmy to introduce the next act.

Timmy was not happy to be cut off before his set was over, and he screamed, "Oh, the order of wings is for table five, Ed!"

That actually got a few chuckles from a couple of the tables.

"Give it up for Timmy Conners! If you think he sucks at telling jokes, come in for lunch some time. And make sure you count your wings if he's your waiter!"

The crowd laughed uproariously at that as Timmy left the stage, returning to his real job of waiting on tables. It didn't take him long to get ready to wait on tables, all he had to do was put on a cap and a t-shirt with the name of the establishment on it. He approached a table with three men dressed in business suits, looking at the menu.

"Hey, guys!" he said, "Welcome to the Sports Shack. I'll be taking your order." Timmy paused for a moment and said, "Hey, I think I went to school with you guys!"

The men put down their menus, looked at each other,

and then rolled their eyes. One of them said, "You went to school with us? I don't know about that."

Timmy didn't seem to get the obvious sarcasm. "Yeah. Timmy. Timmy Conners! I do standup here. I only help out waiting tables when someone doesn't show up for work. I think I was like a year ahead of you guys. And I know your sister had a crush on me," Timmy said, pointing to one of three.

"I don't think my sister ever stooped that low, Tommy!" the businessman said as he looked at the other two guys.

"It's Timmy! And, you know, I think you're right. This girl had more teeth than your sister had. And she weighed about a hundred pounds less, too!" Timmy said as he chuckled under his breath.

The businessman started to stand up, but he was held down by the other two.

Timmy finished his shift and went home to his mom's apartment. He took a seat at the card table, and Blanche joined him, putting down a can of Old Milwaukee for him and taking a sip of her own.

"Way to go, moron! Now we got no job! I guess your jokes weren't too funny, eh?" Blanche smirked.

Timmy shrugged his shoulders and said, "I'm glad to be out of that dump! I get twenty bucks to MC, do my act, and clean up afterward! No thanks!"

He took a sip of his beer and said, "I'm gonna work really hard on putting an act together and get the heck outta here! I'll go somewhere where they appreciate good comedy!"

Blanche sipped her beer before going into the kitchen and moving some things around. Then she put some paper plates on the card table with some plastic forks and pulls off a couple of paper towels to serve as napkins.

"So, how's mac and cheese sound for dinner tonight?" she asked.

"Sure. We got any of those little wieners? I like those little wieners with my mac and cheese," he responded.

"Anything else, your highness?" Blanche said sarcastically.

"Well, you could try really hard not to flip any of your ashes in this batch! I almost barfed last time!"

Both of them chuckled at that.

Chapter Six

Let's Get Ready to Rumble!

The 2002 football season was a great year for USC. The Trojans had just won their last game of the year in great fashion. The players, coaches, and trainers were celebrating in the dressing room.

Butch sat half-dressed at his locker after his shower, wearing only his slacks and shoes. He was taking his things out of his locker, gently folding them, and putting them into a backpack. Johnny, the starting linebacker, approached him in a sweat-soaked t-shirt. He hadn't taken off his bottom pads and shoes. He was yelling in cadence with most of the other players about the win and the possibility of their going to a bowl game.

"Wow! Butch, can you believe it, man? We should get that bowl bid now! What do you think? Cotton Bowl? Sugar Bowl? If Oregon loses tonight, we might even get back into the Rose Bowl." Johnny got louder with each statement. "Hey, man, you listening to me?"

"Yeah, man. I'm excited! Look, I think any bowl we get invited to will be great!" Butch said. "I just got a lot going on right now."

Johnny nodded, "Hey, I get ya. All those scouts looking at you! So, we'll see you at Amber's place tonight? Campus cops have already been taken care of, and we got beer kegs galore!"

The last thing Butch put into the backpack was a pair of wrestling tights. He paused for a moment and said, "I got somewhere I gotta be tonight, but I'll try and make it later."

"All right, buddy. We'll see you there!" Johnny said as he slapped Butch on the shoulder and immediately started high fiving the other players near Butch's locker. "Bowl bound, baby!"

Butch finished dressing and exited the exuberant locker room. He made a beeline to his car and dropped his bag in the backseat. As he started the car, he looked at the stadium and the remaining fans who were partying because of the great win. It amazed him how fast his college football career was ending. But the excitement of pursuing a career in professional wrestling was front and center on his mind and was all he could think about.

Butch drove to the San Diego Convention Center where

the California-based All American Professional Wrestling Show was being held. He grabbed his bag from the backseat and walked toward the entrance where the wrestlers could get to the locker room unobstructed by rowdy wrestling fans.

A guard stepped aside and allowed Butch to enter the locker room. He made his way to his locker, put his bag on the chair beside it, and began to get dressed.

Butch looked good in his football uniform, but he looked great in his wrestling outfit. His tights, knee pads, and boots were all brand new. He looked in the mirror and saw how good he looked. A smile began to broaden across his face.

There were about twenty other wrestlers also getting dressed and talking with each other. One of them was older, Jerry Marvell, known as the Magnificent One. He had his championship belt draped over one shoulder, supporting it with one hand, and he had his travel bag over the other shoulder. He moved over to where Butch was getting dressed.

Jerry looked at Butch and said, "You're the new guy, right? Some kinda football superstar!"

Butch knew who Jerry was even though Jerry knew almost nothing about him. He stuck out his hand and said, "Yes sir, I'm the new guy. I'm not so sure about the superstar part. Butch. Butch Vernon."

Jerry didn't shake his hand right away. He was sizing up the new guy. But he eventually shook the newcomer's hand and continued trying to intimidate him. He noticed Butch looking at his championship belt.

"Everybody wants to be the champ! You and every other jobroni in this room wants this belt," he said in a loud voice. "If you think I'm just gonna roll over and let you take this from me, you've got another thing coming. It ain't gonna happen, kid!" he placed his bag on the floor and gently laid his belt across the back of the chair.

Butch really didn't know what to do, so he sat down in his chair as he heard several other wrestlers' chuckle.

Jerry finally broke the coldness of his face with a slight smile and said, "I'm just messing with you, kid. I do that with all the new guys! I've actually heard some great things about you. If what I've heard is true, you'll be wearing this belt soon enough." And he walked over to greet another wrestler with a hug.

Butch breathed a sigh of relief.

One of the promoters, Dino, an overweight Italian, walked into the dressing room. He approached Butch and said, "Hey, Butch, tonight I've got you working as the Masked Avenger. We just want to get you some experience in the ring before we have you working without a hood. I've got you listed as six feet four inches and two hundred and seventy-five pounds. Does that sound right to you?"

Butch nodded in agreement and said, "That works for me. Say, you know about the money, right?"

Dino responded, "Yeah, you don't get paid. Some kinda college thing. I've got it. I've got an envelope for your mom, so make sure she sees me before the night is over."

Dino walked away and then brought another wrestler over to Butch's locker. "Max, I've got you working with Butch tonight."

Butch stood up and shook hands with Max.

"You guys are doing a ten-minute Broadway. That's a draw, Butch. Butch, you're the baby face. Max, bring some heat for the first couple of minutes, and then, Butch, do some power stuff. Let's make it a great show, boys!"

During the match, Butch made his share of mistakes in the ring, but he looked so good to the crowd that it really didn't stand out to them. His first match was a success.

Butch continued to work his way up the wrestling ladder until he finally got the belt. Butch finally became the world champ. His childhood dream became a reality!

Chapter Seven

Welcome Back!

A lot of people have no desire to return to the high school from which they graduated. Butch, however, was one who really looked forward to returning to a place that held so many fond memories. He was backstage, waiting to address the students. The hometown hero returns!

Butch had been in the spotlight so much that being here didn't really make him nervous. But, as he waited, his heartbeat began to elevate as he anticipated facing two thousand students waiting to hear what he had to say.

Principal Hedges stood at the podium and addressed the students in a boring tone, occasionally checking his notes as he spoke. Seated behind him were several teachers and administrators. One of those seemed to stand out from the others. Meghan looked more like a model than a teacher; she was certainly easy on the eye. The principal was finishing up the announcements before introducing the returning hero.

"One last announcement. There won't be any after-school activities this Tuesday as we are having the parking lot repaved. So, make sure you make other plans for that day."

He put his notes away and the boring tone left his voice.

"Now, the reason we are assembled here today. We've got a real treat for you. We're honored to have a champion athlete, a great student, and just an all-round great guy who happens to be a graduate of our fine school." He turned and smiled as he looked at Butch. "So, without further ado, help me give a big Tiger Creek High School welcome to our very own Anthony "Butch" Vernon!"

As soon as the introduction concluded, Butch kissed his cross necklace, walked toward the podium, and received a standing ovation from the teachers and students. The auditorium was filled with a raucous roar. For a moment he stood there, looking very much the picture of success in expensive dress shoes, tailored dress slacks, a silk dress shirt, a designer sports coat, and his championship belt draped over his shoulder. For the benefit of the assembly, he proudly displayed the belt over his head.

He acknowledged the applause and cheers and turned to the principal, teachers, and administrators behind him and shook hands with as many as he could. Everyone said something, but when he got to Meghan, he could only make eye contact with her and hold her hand. He couldn't help it, and his face said "Wow!" to her.

The trance was broken by the principal calling his name and waving for him to return to the podium. Once he was in position, Butch addressed the students.

"Thank you, Principal Hedges, teachers, administrators, and students. I'm not here to talk about the things I do in the ring or how I won this," and he paused to hold up the championship belt again. "I'm here to talk to you about what I did when I was sitting right where you are sitting now. It seems like just a few short years ago that I was sitting in this auditorium, walking these halls, and playing sports on these very same fields. This is where you will start to make the choices that will shape the rest of your life."

Butch turned around to glimpse at Meghan and give her another smile. She shyly smiled back.

"This," he resumed, "is where you will make the decision to benefit society or be a burden on society. It is my hope and prayer that you will all choose to benefit others."

He placed the championship belt on the podium and pulled out some notes from a coat pocket.

"And so, I'd like to spend the next few moments talking to you about how the choices you are making today will affect everything you do for the rest of your life. But don't worry. I plan on throwing in plenty of wrestling stories!"

The students gave their approval with applause. And for the next half hour they hung on his every word until he concluded, "remember how important all your choices are for your future and remember that all of us," and he pointed to everyone on the stage, "are here for you! There is always someone who will listen to your problems. Thank you and may God richly bless all of you! Thank you!"

His audience acknowledged his presentation with a standing ovation, and Butch backed away from the podium. The teachers and administrators slowly surrounded Butch while hordes of students came to the front to get a picture of the hometown champion.

Butch kept an eye on Meghan, and she kept an eye on him. He even motioned for her to wait as he attempted to get away from the crowd and approach her.

"I don't think it's appropriate for a man to give his number to an attractive woman and ask her to call him when he doesn't even know her name," he said. Thankfully Meghan introduced herself, to which Butch gave a sigh of relief.

"This is my card, Meghan. I wonder if you're willing to make an exception for me. I need to spend some time with these kids, but I would love to see you again, if that is okay with you. Please call me so I can get your number and do this the right way," he said.

Meghan took his card and nodded in agreement.

Butch went back to the podium, picked up his belt, and jumped off the stage to be among the students who had swarmed the front to see him. He posed for pictures and signed autographs until the last student had gone.

As he was leaving the auditorium, he looked at his phone. Meghan had texted him her number along with a smiley face. That brought a smile to Butch's face as he reached his car. He had plans to meet his mother for dinner at a downtown restaurant, and she had texted him that she would get the table.

When he entered the restaurant, the manager greeted him. "Mr. Vernon, so glad to have you back. Jan will show you to your table," and she motioned for the waiter to take him to the dining area in the back, where Butch's mother was waiting.

At the table, Butch leaned over and kissed the top of Sydney's head before he took his seat. He immediately shared with her the whole experience of returning to his alma mater.

Over their salads, Sydney asked, "Did it feel funny walking around Tiger Creek today?"

"You know, it actually felt great!" he said after a sip of water. "I had a real good vibe from the students. Plus, I met someone. She works there."

Sydney smiled and pulled out her phone. "My friends have been calling me all afternoon. Did you forget that I'm in touch with the girls in the office there?"

Butch rolled his eyes and smiled. "I should have known. Your friends can never keep a secret."

Sydney leaned forward, her elbows on the table and her chin on her hands. "So, tell me about her. They said her name is Meghan, right?"

Chapter Eight

Well, We're Moving on Up!

Timmy's dream was slowly becoming a reality. He was now on a professional stage. The marquee outside the venue had the names of a couple of comics, followed by "Plus Other Comics." Timmy was one of the other comics.

But the place was packed with maybe two hundred paying customers, and Timmy—still overweight, but sporting a full beard, a Hawaiian shirt, jeans, and flip-flops—was on stage and in the middle of his routine.

"Yeah, so I'm the 'other' comic your mom warned you about." He changed his voice to a falsetto of a domineering mother. "I don't want you dating that 'other' comic! Can't you get a date with a headliner? I thought I raised you better than that!"

The audience laughed.

"I don't plan on always being the other comic. I hope to

someday work my way up to 'also appearing'! And if I work really hard and show the proper initiative, I can someday become 'the special guest.' I ought to have my driver's license changed to 'also appearing'! I get mail at my place for 'occupant', and the girl at the 7-Eleven always says, 'Hey, you're that guy,' and to the broad who lives upstairs from me, I'm 'that creepy guy who's watching me all the time.' No wonder I'm confused, talk about an 'identity crisis'!"

Timmy finally takes a break from his rant to sip a drink on a nearby stool. He inhales a long drag from a cigarette also on the stool and then resumes his routine.

"Talk about identity crisis, what about that clown we have for a president, Mr. Peanut himself, Jimmy Carter? That guy doesn't know if he's coming or going. Me, I think he needs to go! Folks, I was this close to making the U.S. Olympic ping-pong team, and Grits goes and boycotts the games! So what am I going to do with a basement full of ping-pong stuff? It's a good thing I used my mom's credit card. I can let her worry about it!"

The audience laughs—except for one couple, both of whom look to be in their forties. The man has short hair cut in a military style, and the woman looks very meek and subservient.

Timmy continued his routine.

"And don't get me started on the hostages in Iran! I've got my flight booked to Canada because you're not gonna see my fat rear end in any kind of military uniform! No sir!"

Timmy pretends to answer a phone.

"Hello, White House? Yes, this is him. Uh-huh, uh-huh. So, let's get this straight. You want to trade me for who? Wait a minute! Who is this? Bobby, is that you? You're too funny. Get back to work, you jerk!"

Timmy paces around on the stage, shrugging his shoulders. Then he starts again.

"I tell you what, let's trade some of those stinking politicians for the hostages!"

The audience loves his suggestion, and many hoot and holler and applaud.

But the older guy with the military-style haircut has had all he can handle and stands to his feet. He motions for his wife to stand up. He adjusts his pants and stares at Timmy on the stage. He points his finger at him and says, "Why don't you quit bad-mouthing our country?"

Timmy is thrilled to have a heckler in the crowd.

"I'm sorry, Pops. I don't remember opening the floor for debate! Why don't you sit your tired rear end back down? Or better yet, isn't it way past your bedtime?"

The obvious veteran responds, "I have the right to stand and speak my mind. I fought for my rights—and yours! I don't see you doing anything but running your mouth!"

Timmy looks off stage and says, "Somebody should have told me Patton was dropping by!" Then he looks at the veteran and says, "Hey, Pop, who'd you fight for? The North or the South?"

The audience seems to be getting into the back-and-forth between the comic and the vet. Heads swivel between Timmy and the heckler throughout the exchange.

The vet responds, "I fought for the United States of America. I did that so we could remain a free country and sleep safe in our beds at night. Not so some long-haired punk like you could run it down!"

Timmy applauds in a mocking manner.

"Are you through, Major Downer? This stuff writes itself! I'm not making it up! Have you read a paper lately, Pops? Just what do you expect me to do?"

The vet takes his wife's arm and turns toward the door. "If you don't like the way this country is being run, if you think you can do a better job, then why don't you run for office, and then you can change it!"

The couple exits as the crowd hoots and hollers. But Timmy throws one last jab.

"Hey, Sarge, don't go away mad. Just go away. You people in the back of the room, if you see me drop the mic and run, it means that Pops came back with an M16 and wants to really make his point!"

The audience laughs as Timmy motions to a waitress with a tray of drinks. She approaches the stage, and he takes his time choosing which one he wants. He finally picks one and takes a sip. Then he looks at the waitress.

"Sorry, sweetheart, for taking so long to make up my mind on the drinks. I was looking for one that didn't have any sweat drops from your armpits."

Timmy turns his back to the audience. His hands are shaking as he empties the entire drink. After taking a deep breath, he turns back to the crowd to finish his set.

"So, which sounds better to you guys: Senator Conners or Congressman Conners?"

The crowd yells out their choices while Timmy scratches his head and looks as if he is pondering his choice.

"You know, I really don't see my big butt running for anything. But if I'm gonna run for something, what the heck, it might as well be for president! Who's behind me?"

Timmy throws his arms up in the air and steps out into the audience. The audience stands, applauding, and they shake his hand and pat his back as he makes his way through the crowd.

Chapter Nine

Decisions, Decisions

For the first time in a long time Timmy felt good about how his set went. After it was over, the cleaning crew went to work. Most of the chairs were turned up on the tables, and the only sound was the swish and slop of a mop on the floor.

At one of the tables in the middle of the room, the chairs were still in place. One of the headline comics, Jack E. Springer, sat in front of a glass of milk, with a towel around his neck. Jack was a plain-looking, slender thirty-something.

Timmy appeared from the kitchen, wearing an apron and a hair net and carrying a large tray of food. He approached Jack, plopped down a large salad, and then he joined him. Timmy's plate has a steak, loaded baked potato, and a handful of French fries. He pulled out a bottle of ketchup from one pocket and a beer from the other.

Jack was surprised that Timmy invited himself to sit down. In his stage voice he said sarcastically, "Yeah, go ahead and sit down. Don't mind me."

Timmy doesn't get the sarcasm.

"They usually don't let me eat here," he said and then pointed to the steak, "but this one was dropped on the floor, so I figured, what the heck, they're just going to throw it out!"

Jack cast a disgusted look at the food on Timmy's plate.

"You ever think about maybe cutting back on the high fat and carbs? You know, a salad every once in a while, wouldn't kill you."

"I went to the clinic for some blood work, and they told me I needed to cut this out and that out and stop smoking and start exercising," Timmy said with a mouthful of potato and some sour cream dripping down his chin.

"So, what'd you do?" Jack asked.

"I kept going to different doctors until I found this fat old turd who was in worse shape than me. He told me I'm young and I can eat whatever the heck I want! That's my kinda doctor!" Timmy said, wiping his mouth and taking a drink of his beer.

Jack shook his head and picked up a fork. "Freaky weird crowd tonight, right?"

Timmy nodded. "Yeah. Was that a kick in the gut or what?"

"You should see if you can get that vet to come back every night. You got some real heat with him!" Jack said as he wiped his mouth.

"You're telling me! So what'd you think?" Timmy asked.

"Think?" Jack seemed confused. "Think about what?"

"About the gimmick tonight. You know. Me running for president!"

Jack sat up with a surprised look. "Ah, are you serious? I thought you were just working the crowd a bit."

With a serious tone Timmy said, "That's how it started out. But then I got to thinking. And bam! It hit me! We've had crooks, perverts, and complete idiots in the White House. What makes them so special?"

"Well, for one thing, I think they had some kind of idea of how government works," Jack said.

Feeling more and more animated, Timmy responded, "Please! I'd be doing it for the press, and maybe it would help me with the ladies, if you know what I mean. What? I gotta fill out a few forms, pay a couple thousand bucks, maybe pee in a cup, and boom, I'm running for president!" He picked up his raw steak with both hands and took a huge bite out of it.

"If anything, maybe I'll get a blurb on the six o'clock news. Think what that would do for business."

Jack returned to his salad and acted like he was listening to Timmy. A moment later he said, "I'm glad you're not thinking about winning. I don't think you could pass the physical."

Timmy, with a little sour cream and potato on his face and some ketchup on his apron, laughed.

"Yeah, ha ha, me on a treadmill. That would be something!"

All of sudden he began to choke on something, and then he coughed it up and farted at the same time. He spat a piece of steak into his hand and wiped his mouth but kept whittling away at the food on his plate.

Jack, however, had heard enough. He pushed his salad away and leaned as far back from the table as possible and said, "You're a real presidential piece of work, Timmy Conners."

Chapter Ten

The World Record

When the next election rolls around, Timmy is once again up to no good, pretending to be running for president. A year earlier, a new twenty-four-hour comedy cable station premiered called That's Funny. They feature up-and-coming comedians as well as some of the best in the business, such as Richard Pryor, George Carlin, and Rodney Dangerfield. Since they were a new channel, they were hungry for programming. Bennie Taylor, a young staffer, happened to catch Timmy's show at the comedy club. Bennie was returning to New York and decided to stay overnight at a motel near the club. On what would turn out to be a rare occurrence, Timmy was really funny that night.

When Bennie returned to New York, he pitched Timmy at that week's production meeting. He had played a tape of Timmy's act and the audience's response, and very quickly the group was laughing along with the crowd.

One of the bosses even knew a little about Timmy Conners. "Say, isn't that the bozo who runs for president every election year?" Some of the other staffers seemed to know bits and pieces of the story.

"You know," the boss said, "I think we need to send a camera crew to Conners' next gig and see if we can get enough for a segment whenever we need some filler!"

They assigned the task to Bennie. It was his first real assignment.

A couple of weeks later, Bennie and a cameraman named Sid showed up at Timmy's club, unannounced. Bennie was hoping for a great night of comedy, because no one wants to bomb out on their first assignment.

As they made their way through the bar area of the club, past the stage and into the back offices, which were next to the restrooms and a broom closet, they saw a handwritten sign taped to the door: "Conners for President Head."

Bennie and Sid cracked up at the sign. They listened for a moment outside the door to hear if there were any signs of life inside. Instead, they recoiled at the sound of one of the loudest farts they had ever heard.

"Oh, yeah," Timmy laughed, "now that's the sound a

turd makes when it's heading for the tunnel! Coming through . . . outta my way! I gotta use that one tonight. I hope I didn't crap my pants!"

Bennie knocked on the door.

"Hold on . . . Hold on . . . Let me get my pants on!" Timmy says as he zips up.

A moment later he swings the door open, and the odor knocks the two men back a step. While Timmy finishes tucking his shirt in, he asks, "Can I help you guys?"

Sid pulls his large camera to his shoulder and starts rolling tape.

"Hi, Timmy?" Bennie says. "Timmy Conners, right?"

The comedian is stunned and takes a step back.

"Look, uh, she told me she was twenty-one. Uh, she looked twenty-one. That's the only reason we served her a drink."

"No, Mr. Conners," Bennie says. "We're with That's Funny, the comedy channel. We want to do a story on you and your run for the presidency."

Timmy shrugged his shoulders. "Oh, yeah, yeah. Sure. I knew that! I'm jerking your chain man! Whew. That's Funny? Yeah, I've watched that. I get some of my best stuff from you guys. Just kidding. Good shows!" After a slight pause, he adds, "So, just to get this straight, Melissa's father didn't send you guys, right?"

Bennie laughs. "Oh, man, you are hilarious. Look, can we talk to you?"

"Sure, no problem. Say, are you guys hungry? The grill here does a wicked chili-covered dog." Timmy says and then lets out another huge fart.

Bennie and Sid both take a step back.

"That's from this morning's dog!" Timmy says. "See what I mean? Wicked or what?"

Bennie says, "Well, maybe we'll have a grilled cheese or something light."

"Suit yourselves. Come on, we'll grab a table. But wait a minute. I gotta do something real quick. Stay here. I'll be right back." And then Timmy disappears into his office.

A moment later he reappears with another handwritten note. "This is perfect! Perfect! Can you film me while I put this on the men's john?"

He holds the paper up, and Bennie and Sid both read "Please do not flush! Possible world's record! Awaiting confirmation!"

Sid was confused. "So, the toilet's broken?"

"Nah," Timmy said. "The thing works just fine. But I took a crap in there earlier, and I'm pretty sure it's some kind of record. I called the Guinness people, but I just got their machine."

Timmy looks at Sid. "If you could film this beast that would help validate it."

The New Yorkers look at each other, and Bennie changes the subject.

"Oh, man, we'd love to," he says, "but we only have enough film for your show tonight."

Timmy was disappointed but not discouraged. "That's okay, this thing could be big! You know, like that snake-lizard thing over in England!"

Bennie isn't sure what Timmy is talking about, but he takes a guess. "You mean the Loch Ness Monster?"

"Yeah, yeah," Timmy says. "Or even as big as Bigfoot! I could call this thing Bigturd! I could charge like a couple of bucks a head to come see it. I could even make up t-shirts and have a Bigturd day in town or something!"

Timmy turned toward the men's room.

"We'll just meet you at the grill!" Bennie said.

A little later, Timmy, his mouth covered with chili sauce, takes a moment away from eating to show Bennie and Sid that he understands why they're there.

"So, you want to do a segment on me and how every four years I run for president? Yeah, sure. But don't forget the most important part. I can get some free t-shirts, right?" And then he inhaled the last bite of his dog.

"Even better, Timmy! You'll get paid! And not just

once, but every time it airs. We'll send you a check," Bennie explained.

"Can we do cash?" Timmy asked sheepishly.

"No, it has to be a check. It's a business thing," Bennie said.

"Well, I'll give you my ex-wives' addresses, and you guys can fight with them as to who gets what! So, you want to start tonight?"

"Yeah, that's the plan. Maybe we follow you around town, see you interact with some of the locals. Then catch your show and do a few backstage interviews?"

Timmy shakes his head. "Yeah, I really don't go into town much. There's a couple of places I'm, well, let's just say I'm not allowed to go back for some reason or another. I tell you what, you guys go into town, snoop around. You know, ask around about me. See how the locals feel, and in the meantime, I'm going to take a little power nap. You know, recharge the old batteries!"

Timmy slams his hands down on the table, proud of his campaign decision. He stands up from the table, holding his belly. "I'll just catch up with you guys before the show. Right now, I got a turd whistling for the right of way!"

He leaves the table, and Bennie wonders what he's gotten himself into, hoping he and Sid find enough to put something together for New York.

That night Bennie and Sid sit front and center at the comedy club when Timmy walks onstage wearing a cloth diaper and nothing else. The small crowd applauds and starts to laugh. Sid starts filming as Timmy stands center stage and grabs the microphone.

"Good evening, all you fine people. Thanks for coming out tonight. Before I get started, I want to let you know that we're being filmed tonight for the new comedy channel That's Funny." He points to Sid.

"So, for a change, I'm going to try and be funny tonight. You may be wondering about my outfit." Timmy pauses and models his homemade diaper, turning 360 to give the crowd a full view.

"Well, I had a little issue earlier today, and I started thinking, what if I'm actually out in public, or even worse, what if I'm working like an eight-to-five job and, well, you know, nature and a dozen hot wings and a fifth of vodka start to kick in! Bingo! I wear this!" He points to his diaper. "I don't have to excuse myself from a meeting. I don't have to run to the nearest john and hope I make it in time. I just play it cool and let it flow."

The crowd laughs.

"In fact, I think I feel today's lunch coming down the tunnel!" Timmy pauses and gets a sour look on his face, shivers a little, then shakes his leg. "Nah, just kidding folks!"

"Yeah, you guys in the front row may want to move back some. I'm giving that one about thirty seconds before it hits you in the face like a dead carp!"

Again, the crowd laughs...

After the show, Bennie and Sid interview some of the audience members.

"So, what do you think of Timmy's act?"

"Would you vote for him as president?"

An older man in denim overalls says, "Well, anybody who can wear a diaper in front of a crowd and not let it bother them, I'd vote for that! He's a straight shooter, that's for sure!"

A group of twenty something women say, "He's rude, obnoxious, disgusting, foul, and an idiot!" Then one of the girls adds, "So he'd make a perfect president!" And they all laugh.

A few weeks later That's Funny airs the piece on Timmy. It's one of their highest-rated shows of the season.

Timmy and some of the clubs' workers are gathered at the bar, watching the show as Bennie signs off.

"This has been Bennie Taylor with an inside look at the presidential campaign of independent candidate Timmy Conners. God help us if this man ever gets elected to any political office!"

After the show, Timmy gets a few high-fives from his employees.

"Great job, boss!"

"You killed it, man!"

"You're a TV star now, Timmy!"

The comedian just smiles, soaking it all in.

Chapter Eleven

Butch Keeps His Morals

Wrestling in Japan has always been a great treat for American wrestlers. Japan is a wonderful and beautiful country. The people are very kind. And the money one can make in Japan is always a great thing too!

Butch was there to wrestle for the first time. The Japanese All Star Wrestling League was one of the best. Their reputation as a first-class organization was widely known throughout the wrestling world. Butch was excited to be there. They were very excited to have the American champion in their country.

Usually, the smallest crowd the wrestlers would work in front of in Japan is about seventeen thousand. Butch was working in one of their largest venues on this night. There were giant posters on the walls and hallways of the arena. Many of the posters had Butch's picture front and center.

In the locker room were twenty-something Japanese wrestlers. They were smaller than the American wrestlers, and many of them wore masks and flashy costumes. The average size of the Japanese wrestlers was around five feet eight, weighing about 185 pounds.

Butch picked a quiet spot in the back of the locker room that gave him plenty of space to change. He was sitting in a chair shirtless but still wearing his dress slacks and shoes. His wrestling gear was neatly laid out beside him. His championship belt was draped across the back of the chair.

Butch used the nearby pay phone to call Meghan. It was difficult for him to hear. He pressed the phone tightly against one ear and used his free hand against his other ear so he could hear what she was saying.

"Yes, dear. I'm being a good boy. There's not really much for me to do here other than wrestle and travel to the next arena."

He pressed the phone tighter against his ear. "No. The language barrier is a real problem. Yesterday I asked for a chicken sandwich, and they brought me something squishy that had eyes bugging out at me. I can't wait to get home, sweetie."

The noise in the locker room increased, and Butch said, "I miss you too, Meghan. . . . Yes, I love you too! See you soon!"

Just as Butch ended the call, the Japanese promoter, Miko Tannaka, and the guy Butch is going to work against, both about one foot shorter and a hundred pounds smaller than Butch, approach him and bow.

"Ah, Mr. Butch, this is Sooni Jakanaki, he very good wrestler. He no speak good English, so I help him work it out with you!"

Butch returned the bow. He knew this would be a long night.

The match actually went better than he had anticipated. Most Japanese wrestlers are great workers, and Sooni was no exception. The crowd obviously loved the match by the tremendous sound that filled the arena.

After the match, Butch was in the locker room, attempting to unwind. He was wearing his slacks and had a towel around his neck. As he bent over to tie his shoes, the promoter approached. As Miko bowed, smiling, Butch could see he was closely followed by two beautiful women, both of whom were dressed to impress.

Miko extended an envelope to Butch, containing his payment for a great match. The American accepted it and placed it in his coat pocket, not bothering to check the payment.

The promoter smiled and said, "Great match, Mr. Butch. We all very happy you wrestle for us."

Butch smiled, "It was my pleasure, Mr. Tannaka. You might want to have your boy's shoulder looked at, though. That was a pretty hard bump he took out there."

Miko smiled and nodded again, perhaps not understanding what Butch had said. He moved to the side and lifted his hand toward the two women, like a game show host, showing off the winning prize. He motioned for them to step forward.

"Mr. Butch, these are for you."

The two women bowed to Butch and smiled.

Butch, however, wasn't sure what the promoter meant.

"Mr. Tannaka, I already have a driver, and all my meals are taken care of. What are these girls for?"

Now it was Miko's turn to be confused. He looked at the girls, then at Butch. He smiled and gave Butch a wink. Then he bent down to Butch's ear and whispered while pointing at the girls.

After a few words, Butch's demeanor changed from a smile to a frown and a raised eyebrow. When Miko finished, he backed away and gestured toward the women again.

Butch stood to his feet, removed the towel from his neck, and put on his shirt, missing a few buttons as he hurriedly dressed. He walked toward the two women, taking each one by the arm, and gently escorted them to the door of the dressing room. He opened the door and motioned for them to leave. Then he turned to face Miko with a grimace after he shut the door.

Miko looked confused as Butch approached. Butch said, "Mr. Tannaka, I'm not sure how you do business here, but I do not appreciate your offer. It would be to your benefit to stop doing this type of thing when it comes to me, especially if you ever want me to wrestle for you again. Do you understand me?"

The promoter bowed and exited apologetically. Butch turned around, shaking his head. Without saying another word, Butch finished packing his gear and made a bee-line for his ride, purposely avoiding any contact with the others.

Chapter Twelve

Let the Campaign Begin!

Amazingly, Timmy worked his way up to being a headliner of the comedy club circuit. But even as a headliner, he still had to do a lot of his own stage preparation. Fortunately, today he had a couple of young club staffers to help him set up: Steve and Dene. Dene was a beautiful, twenty-something blonde wearing jogging shorts and a midriff T-shirt.

Timmy walked on the stage with a large rolled-up banner. He was singing and whistling and very excited about his routine for the evening. He unfurled the banner across the stage floor and looked at Steve and Dene who appeared to be puzzled.

"I've been waiting for this sucker for months!" he said. "Now I feel like my campaign is official! I've got a banner!"

But neither Dene nor Steve had any idea what he was

talking about.

"What's this got to do with us? I thought we were going to be working today!" Dene said sarcastically.

"You are working, dear," Timmy said. "I'm going to need you two to hang up this banner for me. Now grab this end, Steve. Dene, you grab the other end." But his attention was fixated on Dene.

"So, sweetheart, what I'm gonna have you do is grab this end and take it up that ladder over there. You see the ropes in the ringlets? You and Steve are going to tie them to the poles on each side of the stage."

Timmy smiled as Dene walked toward the ladder, and he followed behind very closely. As she was going up the ladder, Timmy put his hands around her waist to help.

"I'm just trying to help you, sweetie. Sure don't want you to fall and hurt yourself," he said with a smile on his face.

Timmy had placed the ladder just far enough from the pole so that Dene would have to lean over to tie the ropes. As she did, his eyes were focused on her, not the banner.

"How does this look?" Dene asked.

"Oh, baby, that looks great!" Timmy said slowly.

She said, "I'm talking about the banner, you pervert!"

After Dene came down from the ladder, Steve took it over to the other side of the stage and said, "Hey, can I get some help on this end?"

But Timmy's eyes were fixed on Dene. "You're on your own over there, chum. I've got my hands full here."

After the banner was tied up, the three of them walked to the center of the stage to see how it looked. They took in the huge bold letters: "Conners for President." All of them tilted their heads to the same side when they noticed the banner was crooked—kind of like Timmy.

Timmy looked at Dene and said, "Well, darlin', you did great. Your end looks fantastic! I see big things in your future."

Then he looked at Steve and said, "But you suck, man! Your end of the banner is crooked!"

Timmy placed his arm around Dene's shoulders and began to walk her off the stage.

"You did so great, sweetie, let me buy you a beer to show my appreciation!"

Steve just stood there with his head down.

After the banner was leveled, Timmy went to his dressing room to get ready for his set. A few minutes later the manager walked in.

"Hey, Conners, I got some complaints about you from the two who were helping earlier. Dene doesn't ever want to be around you again, and Steve had a nervous breakdown."

"I don't know what their problem is, Frank. I just wanted the banner to look great for my routine tonight!" Timmy said as he finished dressing.

"You're on first tonight, fat boy!" the manager said as he turned to leave.

"Wait a minute, Frank. I'm a headliner. Why do I have to go on first?" Timmy complained.

"Well, Brainiac, your banner is up there. Nobody else wants your stinking banner up there during their routines. Just do your job and quit whining," Frank said as he slammed the door behind him.

Timmy wore white pants, a blue shirt, and a red blazer. The first part of his routine went great. He was wowing them as he passed out little American flags to the audience.

"So after fifteen minutes of yelling at this guy, I realized he was talking about taxes, not Texas! Man, did I feel like an idiot!"

The audience laughed and applauded. His routine seemed to get better and better as it went on. Again, the audience applauded and hooted and hollered loudly.

"Thank you! Thank you! You've been a great crowd! That's why I'm honored to kick off my campaign fund-raising right here and now! You guys are the best!"

He gestured and a young woman joined him onstage. She had dyed red hair, too much makeup, a trench coat, and white high-heel boots. She was holding a red-white-and-blue top hat.

The men in the crowd were obviously interested in Timmy's companion.

"Ladies and gentlemen, this is Trixie Trix. Miss Trix comes to us from the famous Boom-Boom Room, where she does two shows nightly. I was so impressed with her show, I decided she would be perfect at helping me launch my campaign," he said.

Then he grabbed the shoulders of her trench coat and pulled it off to show she was wearing a very small red-white-and-blue bikini. Trixie was going to use the top hat to collect donations. Timmy helped her step down to the floor.

"So dig deeply in your pockets and purses for your donations! Remember, the more you give, the happier that makes Trixie—if you know what I mean!"

As Trixie walked through the crowd, people—mostly men—reached into their pockets and dropped bills into the hat. And she acknowledged every donation by doing little jumps for joy.

"That's right, folks, give till it hurts! And remember,

your donations are probably tax deductible." After a little pause he added, "I may need to look into that."

Chapter Thirteen

Breakfast for Champions

Butch loved working out. He loved the feeling he had after a hard workout. This day was no exception. After he had finished, he put on some clean sweats, wrapped a towel around his neck, and checked his phone. Sydney had left a message about picking up a few items from the grocery store on his way home. Butch didn't mind getting what she needed and dropping her items off on his way to his apartment.

A half hour later, Butch was steering a cart toward the fruits and vegetables section. As he turned down an aisle, he saw a young mother and her little boy were blocking the way. The woman didn't notice Butch, but her son sure did. His eyes widened and locked onto the champ.

Butch noticed the boy's stare and he walked over to

him and knelt down.

"Are you staring at me? Do you know who I am?" Butch said in a menacing voice.

The boy's eyes grew even wider, his mom realized they were no longer alone in the aisle, and then she recognized him. She put her arm around her son, and the boy said, "Yes sir! You're Butch Vernon! The wrestler!"

Still using his serious voice, Butch responded, "That's right! And what is your name, little man?"

The boy's mom smiled as she looked down at her son and responded, "This is Max, and I'm his mom, Nancy. I'm a little amazed this little guy knows you. He's never met a famous athlete before."

Butch reached out his hand. "Put it there, Max. I am so pleased to meet you. I was just messing with you. The day I can't stop and talk to a fan, especially a young fan, is the day I need to start looking for something else to do for a living."

He stood and tried to think of something he could give Max. So, Butch pulled the towel from around his neck and gave it to him.

"Here ya go, Max. Your very own Butch Vernon sweat-drenched workout towel!"

Max smiled from ear to ear. He wrapped the towel around his neck and looked up for his mom's approval. Nancy wasn't as thrilled with the sweaty towel but thanked

Butch for his generosity.

"Thank you, Mr. Vernon. We don't want to take up any more of your time. We've got some more shopping to do," she said as she pulled Max away from Butch.

Butch waved goodbye to Max, and then turned back toward his cart. A familiar box of cereal caught his eye because his picture was on the box.

He quickly turned around and called out, "Miss Nancy, could you wait a moment? I have something else I'd like to give Max."

Butch grabbed a box and walked it over to Max and handed it to him.

"I just remembered I made the cover. Do you happen to have a marker on you, Miss Nancy?"

She opened her purse and pulled out a pen and handed it to him. "Would this pen work?"

While Butch began to write on the box, Nancy said to Max, "Wow, your own autographed box. That's exciting!"

Butch said, "Max, let me read you what I wrote: 'To my good friend, Max, a true champ! Butch Vernon.'"

When Butch handed the new collectible cereal box to him, Max said, "Wow! This is too cool! Thank you so much, Mr. Vernon!"

"You're welcome, Champ!" Butch answered. "I sure

hope you and your mom have a great rest of the day!"

Nancy responded, "That's so sweet of you. Thank you so much!"

Butch gave her pen back to her, reached into his pocket, and gave her a five-dollar bill.

Confused, Nancy asked, "What's that for?"

Butch smiled, "It's for the cereal. I don't expect you to pay for it." And he turned his cart back down the aisle.

Chapter Fourteen

Ding Dong, the Bells are Gonna Chime

Butch was on top of the world. His career in the ring was going great. He was offered roles in movies, and he was getting closer and closer to Meghan. Today would make him feel even more on top of the world.

Butch was being interviewed by Tom O'Malley, who hosted the most popular afternoon television show in the country. Butch looked like a million bucks in his favorite suit, with his championship belt draped across his lap for the interview.

As O'Malley was wrapping up the interview, he said, "Thanks so much for coming by. I know you're a busy man. Looks like we can see you in New York, Philadelphia, Atlanta, and Miami in the coming weeks."

"That's right, Tom. Make sure you get your tickets

early. Thanks so much for having me on your show. It's always a pleasure to see you!" Butch said as he reached out to shake the host's hand.

"Before I forget, did you happen to bring anyone with you this afternoon? I know you usually bring a crowd!" O'Malley said coyly.

Butch pointed into the audience and said, "Well, I've got my mom and my girlfriend out there somewhere."

The house lights came on, and Sydney and Meghan stood up and waved to Butch.

O'Malley said, "Wow! You've got two beautiful women with you! Why don't you two ladies join us here onstage?"

Butch stood up and walked to the edge of the stage to offer his hand to Sydney and Meghan. O'Malley greeted both ladies and shook their hands. "You must be Butch's mom. Nice to meet you. And you must be the girlfriend I've heard so much about."

O'Malley turned to Butch and said, "Butch, I understand you have something to say to Meghan. Why don't you take over?"

Butch pulled a small box out of his jacket pocket, dropped to one knee, and looked up at Meghan. He opened the box and said, "Meghan, I love you more than life itself. You're the greatest gift God has given me physically. You complete my life in every way. Would you do me the honor of becoming my wife?"

Meghan's eyes filled with tears of joy. "Yes, yes, of course I'll marry you!"

Butch stood to his feet, and the two of them kissed and hugged as the audience stood to their feet and applauded.

After the show, Butch, Meghan, and Sydney walked to the limo that was to take them to their hotel. The newly engaged couple held hands as Meghan, still looking at her ring, asked, "So, Champ, are there going to be a lot of surprises like this one in our future?"

Sydney offered her two cents. "Meghan, I can honestly say since Butch was a little boy, he has always been full of surprises. But the majority of them were great surprises."

"Well, ladies," Butch interrupted, "I do have one more surprise. I have to go to my gym and take care of a few things before we meet for dinner. I'm sure you two can find a way to keep yourselves occupied until I join you later."

Meghan asked, "Is someone picking you up?"

"No, the driver is going to drop me off on the way to the hotel. I promise I won't be long."

After a short drive, as Butch was getting out of the limo, he said to Meghan, "Now that we're getting married, we're going to have to find a house. I don't think you'll want to live in my office. I mean, it has a bathroom, a kitchenette, and a bed in it, but I don't think you would be too crazy about living in a gym." He leaned down and kissed her before he shut the door. "Love you babe. See you in a few, Mom."

As soon as Butch entered his office/living quarters, he started going through a large stack of mail. Behind his desk was a huge picture of Butch in his wrestling outfit and championship belt. He had named the gym The Champ's Zone.

Marcus, one of his best employees, knocked at the door, "Hey, Champ, I sorted your mail for you. Hope you don't mind."

"Not at all, Marcus. It made it easy for me to see the most important stuff," Butch said as he picked up a magazine with Meghan's picture on the front cover.

"She made the cover again! Jeez, she's on more covers than you are!" Marcus said.

"Throw it on the pile with the others," Butch said.

"Marcus, we'll be with the president tomorrow, and then I've got a few matches over the next week. I might not be back here for about ten days. Can you take care of everything for me until I get back?" Butch asked as he opened some of the mail on his desk.

"Sure thing, Champ. I've gotcha covered. I've gotta get

back out on the floor and make sure the new guy is treating the customers the way you want us to. See you later!" Marcus said and walked out of the office.

Butch finished up at the office and met Sydney and Meghan at the Steak Master's Restaurant, one of the classiest restaurants in the city. Meghan and Sydney told him about the wedding plans they had discussed. They asked for Butch's input, and the girls laughed at some of his suggestions.

After dinner Butch said, "Well, ladies, we really need to get to the hotel. Meghan and I have a big day tomorrow with the president. The limo will be at the front door at 6:30 a.m. I'm bushed and really need to get some rest."

They arrived at the hotel and went to their separate rooms. Butch kissed Meghan good night. "See you at six. We can get some fruit from the downstairs restaurant and some juice before the limo picks us up, if that's okay with you."

"That's fine. I'll see you in the morning," Meghan said, stopping Butch from closing the door. "I just want you to know that I am looking forward to spending the rest of my life with you," she said as she leaned forward to kiss him one more time.

"I'm looking forward to spending the rest of my life

with you too," Butch said as he closed the door.

Chapter Fifteen

Who's the Next Partner?

Amazingly, Timmy's life continued moving up in a positive way. He moved to San Diego, rented an empty space in a strip mall, and turned it into his own club. The brightly lit sign above the door simply said Timmy's Comedy Club.

Just inside the club was a small lobby and a gift shop where patrons could pick up t-shirts with "Conners for President" on them, comedy albums, and other items. A set of double doors separated the lobby from the club. The double doors were guarded by Wilson, a huge African American who wore an ill-fitting uniform. He sat on a stool and opened the door for paying customers as soon as they showed him their tickets.

The club accommodated about two hundred people.

Waitresses wore short shorts and tight-fitting "Conners for President" T-shirts.

During his routines, Timmy wore a Hawaiian shirt and white slacks. He shaved his beard long ago, but he kept the mustache. His hair is styled now, and he does his best to look like TV's Magnum, P.I., Tom Selleck. On both sides of the stage are large "Conners for President" banners.

Timmy still butchers the English language profusely when he's onstage. He keeps a towel handy and often wipes his face and neck.

"Whew, man!" he regularly tells the audience. "I sure wish I could get a crowd like you guys in here every night! What a treat tonight's been for us all here! As you can see by the banners, I'm running for president . . . again!"

The Audience applauds and hoot and holler at Timmy's standard pronouncement.

"Thank you! Thank you! That fossil Reagan is going to be tough to beat, what with his great acting skills and all. But I'll give it my best shot!"

And as part of his finales, Timmy motions for a couple of waitresses to come onstage with him.

"So, since you guys were such a great audience, I wanted to let you be the first to know my choice for my running mate!"

The waitresses carry up something covered with a sheet, one on each side. Between the girls is a cardboard cutout they present to Timmy.

"Thank you, girls, and don't forget to make sure the champagne is on ice in my office."

The girls smile and exit the stage.

Timmy walks over to the cardboard cutout. He places one hand on the sheet and holds a microphone in the other.

"Since there is no way this gentleman would set foot in this dump, I'll have to do the next best thing."

He pulls off the sheet to reveal a life-size cutout of an older man dressed in a dark suit, with one hand raised and the other hand holding an open Bible. "I present to you my running mate for the 1984 election: The Reverend Gerald Briscolli!"

Laughter and applause follow.

"Now, now, I know what you are thinking," Timmy announces. "Why in the world would the honorable, reliable, worldly, Godly Reverend Briscolli agree to be my running mate? I mean, he's on TV, he's written dozens of best-selling books, and he's even been consulted by past presidents!"

He reaches behind the cutout, pulls back a piece of paper, and shows it to the crowd.

"Well, he doesn't actually know he agreed to be my

running mate. But when I asked him for his autograph, well, let's just say he was signing things so fast, I guess he never took the time to read what I put in front of him!" Timmy pauses. "Oops!"

Then he reads from the paper, "I, Gerald Farnsworth Briscolli, being of sound mind and body, do hereby and under no duress voluntarily agree to participate in the presidential election under the terms contained herein. Blah, blah, blah. You know the rest, right folks?"

Timmy puts the paper on the stool and his arm around the cutout of his running mate.

"I figure I'm not doing very good on the religious stuff or doing good with the religious right, but maybe this will score me some points."

Timmy then motions for his staff to join him on stage. A half dozen pretty waitresses and Wilson join him onstage. The waitresses are wearing red-white-and-blue top hats.

"So, who's ready to get this party off to a rockin' start?"

Timmy walks over to a stereo and presses play. Disco music starts thumping.

"Let the fundraising begin! Wilson, tap that keg of Old Milwaukee. Free beer on me, everybody!"

The waitresses mingle with the crowd. People are putting money in the hats. Wilson rolls his eyes and heads off to tap the keg. Timmy puts the microphone down and starts dancing with the cutout of Reverend Briscolli. Basically, a good night was had by all in attendance.

Chapter Sixteen

The Next Candidate Is . . .

In 1989 Timmy took the stage at his club. He wore a white sports jacket with the sleeves rolled up, white cotton slacks, and white loafers with no socks, mimicking Miami Vice's Don Johnson. His hair was longer and slicked back, and he sported a five-day-old beard. In addition to his new look, he had lost some weight. "Conners for President" signs and banners were festooned all over the place.

As he finished his act, he said, "Wow, thanks again. You guys are great!" Then he gestures to his right. Two assistants appear with a draped figure. The cutout is about four and a half feet tall and from what's not covered, it's apparently the figure of a woman.

Timmy places his arm around the cutout. "Well, it's that time again! Election time! Time for me and my running mate to start kissing babies and raising money!"

"Since I'm slowly turning into America's next sex symbol," pausing to emphasize his new look, "I figured my running mate this go-around should be none other than America's number-one relationship expert!"

He pulled away the drape and said, "That's right, none other than America's own Dr. Sally Handover!"

Timmy leaned over, kissed the image of Dr. Handover on her lips and then lifted the cutout and danced around the stage.

"How's this for a running mate, folks? Do I know how to pick 'em or what?"

Six waitresses come onstage at Timmy's signal and face the audience. They all have the customary red-white-and-blue top hats. Timmy walked over to a stereo and pressed PLAY. Loud music reverberates through the small auditorium and the girls begin to mingle with the crowd. Timmy returns to dancing with the cutout as the audience hoots, applauds and reaches into their pockets for their campaign donations.

A few years later, during the 1992 campaign season, Timmy started to get some national exposure with small articles in some counterculture magazines and grocery-store tabloids. One of the most popular tabloids runs a front-page photo with the headline "Son of Bigfoot to Run for President!" But then some reputable news magazines picked up the story, during the lull before the national party conventions, pointing at the lighter side of campaigning. Time magazine's editors decide to run a cover story on the Conners campaign with the questioning headline "The Future of Politics?" The rival news magazine Newsweek answered with a cover headline "Is This Man for Real?"

The publicity was fantastic for Conner's Comedy Club, and Timmy began to receive invitations to the extremely late-night talk shows. After the 1996 presidential campaign, the invitations began to come from the two highly competitive late-night talk shows.

In 1997 Timmy was welcomed to The Evening Show with David Ledbetter. He was the number-two guest after getting bumped from his first appearance when the dumb-pets segment ran long. Timmy wore a casual dress shirt, dress slacks, and a dinner jacket. his hair was short and neat, though he still has a five-day-old beard.

"Welcome back, folks. We're here with presidential candidate Timmy Conners." Ledbetter paused for a moment before saying, "Timmy, this past election was like your third or fourth time running for president, right?"

"David, it was actually the fifth time I threw my hat into the ring. And as I'm preparing for my sixth, I'd like to ask you to start calling me Tim. That's who I am now: Tim Conners."

Ledbetter rolled his eyes and glanced down at his notes. "You know, Timmy—pardon me—I meant to say Tim. I remember some of your escapades from the eighties. You were quite the entertainer back then. Have you settled down a little now?"

Timmy looked out at the audience, smiled, and said, "Well, David, I've never shied away from talking about the substance abuse problems I had in the past—and the fact that I've been married several times."

The host responded, "And how many Mrs. Conners have there been?"

Timmy counted on his fingers. "I'm on number four now! I think I'm finally getting this marital bliss thing down."

"Well, good luck with that," Ledbetter said. "So, president again? Haven't you beaten that horse to death?"

Timmy finds the active camera and leans toward it. "The way I look at it, I'm an everyday guy. I'm your neighbor. I'm the guy down the street. I'm the guy you grab a beer with after work. So, who better than me to be a candidate for president of the United States?"

The audience applauds, and Timmy sits back and smiles.

"So, you've actually been able to get on the ballot and get votes?"

"Would you be surprised if I told you there are more than a million people in America who are so fed up with the stuffed suits the mainline parties put forth and prop up, that they actually vote for yours truly?"

Ledbetter raises his eyebrows. "I've gotta say that number surprises me. Yes!"

Timmy turns on his comic mode. "Don't get me wrong! I'm still looking to put butts in the seats of my comedy club." He looks into the camera and says, "That's the Conners Comedy Club at 1459 La Mesa Boulevard in the city."

The audience laughs because they know what's coming. Timmy reaches into his coat and pulls out a folded piece of paper. As he opens it, he looks at the audience and smiles.

"David, I know my supporters are chomping at the bit to find out who my running mate is going to be. So, on national television, I'd like to announce to America my running mate for the 1996 election..." He looks at the audience with a big smile and says, "Get ready with a drum roll if you don't mind, George. After twenty-eight years as a late-night ratings competitor, on another station that shall remain nameless, your chief rival has decided to retire!

Plus, I figure he's going to get bored after a couple of weeks and is going to need a new challenge."

The audience really gets into it and hoots, hollers, and cheers.

Timmy reads from the paper: "I, Donald Hawkins, being of sound mind and body, do hereby and under no duress, agree to the terms—" He folds up the paper and says, "Blah, blah, blah. You know the rest!"

The show band starts to play "Hail to the Chief" as balloons and confetti begin to fall onto the crowd.

Timmy and the host stand up, and Timmy acknowledges the applause, which is initiated by Ledbetter. After a moment, the two men return to their chairs, and the host stifles his chuckles and says, "I have to ask, Tim, are you sure Donny's okay with this?"

Timmy laughs out loud and says, "Well, I'm hoping you might help me out on that one since you know him so much better than I. Any chance you might give me his number so I can call him and let him know what he signed a few weeks back?"

The audience loves every minute of the show.

In 2001, after the inauguration of the new president, Timmy does a television commercial for a fried chicken fast-food chain. He is dressed as a chef, and the set is a replica of a front counter of the restaurant. Behind him is a menu board, and positioned nearby is a very fat cat known as the Chicken King Cat. As Timmy finishes his last line, the camera zooms in on the cat, who delivers the closing lines.

"And remember, if the Chicken King don't like it, it ain't no good for you! The Chicken King Cat wants you to eat at Chicken King and vote for Tim Conners for President!"

In 2008, just before the nominating conventions began, Timmy announced his running mate. He appears onstage at the comedy club in an all-white tennis outfit and headband. The cutout is presented to the audience, and the drape is pulled away to reveal the African American pro tennis player Lester Johnson. Timmy pretends to volley with the cutout.

In 2012 Timmy presented another cutout presentation of his running mate. Timmy wears an all-white uniform with white gloves and a white service hat. The cutout figure is American astronaut Randall Hughes in a space suit, complete with helmet. Timmy salutes the cutout and then, as always, he gestures for his waitresses to mingle with the crowd to collect donations.

Timmy smiles at the crowd. "Folks, if you had told me

thirty years ago that my campaign would reach the heights it has today, I wouldn't have believed it. Thanks for your donations. You're making a big difference in your country. And you're showing just how crazy things are in the good old USA! God bless you and God bless America!

Chapter Seventeen

Time to Really Go to Work

In 2016 Timmy has a campaign office in the same strip mall as his comedy club. The office is cluttered with signs and banners. He sits behind a desk, and his hair color has changed to various shades of gray. Timmy has added additional staff because of his rising popularity.

Across from him is his campaign manager, Ron Hillman. He looks much older than he is, an indication of the kind of stress he's under by dealing with people like Timmy. Ron wears a suit and no tie. The two are going over campaign strategies. Ron has a legal pad in his lap, and Timmy throws a rubber ball in the air and occasionally bounces it off the ceiling.

"Tim, I hope you understand the severity of the situation you, I mean, we, are in. All these years you've been running for office, collecting contributions and hiding the money."

Timmy looks at him. "You've done a great job of keeping me out of jail so far. What's the problem?"

"Our problem, Tim, is the enormous sums of money the campaign has coming in. Tim, I can only hide so much!"

"So, what's your suggestion?"

"Well, for one thing, you need to actually spend some money on a campaign!" Ron flips through the legal pad. "Let's start with buying some national airtime. We can produce our own commercials and radio spots. Then we can look at paying salaries for full-time staffers. Plus, I need to know who your running mate is for the campaign. Like now! Ron shook his head and said, "Tim, I need you to be serious for once. We're going to have to do things legitimately. You're going to have to begin paying your staff."

Timmy gets a little peevish. "What's the matter with the staff I have? I pay them!"

He has a half dozen dancers answering the phones (their day job) and working on computers. They're also doing their nails and flipping through magazines. He also has a handful of college interns. Actually, they just watch the dancers. Everybody wears Conners for President t-shirts.

Ron, feeling slightly agitated, says "You can't just bring

anybody in here and call them an employee. Besides, giving them cash and no paperwork isn't exactly legal!"

"You know Ron, for once I agree with you about the money," Timmy says. "You take care of that. Get back to me in a couple of days, and I'll let you know who my running mate is going to be. I promise!"

Ron rolls his eyes. "Yeah, sure."

Timmy walked over to the comedy club. Several people are preparing for the weekend shows. They are setting up tables and chairs, adjusting lights, and hanging the latest campaign signs. Timmy takes a seat at the bar and nibbles on some cherries. He watches the work progress until he notices it's almost dinnertime.

"Say, who wants to grab some grub?"

Everyone stops working for a minute, and Amber, one of the girls, says, "We usually just grab something here."

Timmy makes a face, "Are you kidding? I wouldn't make death-row inmates eat this crap!"

He goes back to the bar and sticks his hand in the tip jar, pulling out a wad of bills. Timmy pockets the money and turns back to the kids.

"Come on! I'm buying! Let's all cram into the Daewoo and see how the other half lives downtown!"

The group starts to file out. Timmy stops Sara, an attractive girl in a tight outfit, and tells her, "You sit up front with me, sweetie!"

At the same time one of the boy's shouts, "Shotgun!"

Timmy shoots him down. "Awe, man, Sara already called it! And rules are rules."

As they're leaving, Ron comes into the room. He and Timmy do a little dance, with Timmy trying to get out and Ron blocking him. Timmy finally gives up.

"Tim, I have a few more things we need to address. We need to talk right now!"

"Wait a minute, Ron." He looks out at the kids. "All right, you win!"

To Ron he says, "I'd love to stay and chat with you, but I gotta feed these brats. Lost a bet!"

"Tim, we need to talk now!"

"I know. I know. Look, I'll be back in like a couple of hours. Five at the most. Then we'll talk. Okay?"

Timmy grabs Ron by the shoulders and moves him out of the doorway. "But right now, I've got my next ex-wife cooking in my Daewoo. So, you'll have to excuse me!"

"Tim, I've been after you for two weeks about your running mate. I've got to have that name so I can leak it to the press."

Timmy pauses in the doorway. "Yeah, I know! Look, it just hasn't hit me yet! I'm waiting for a sign. You know, from above!" And he points at the ceiling.

"From God?"

"No, from the slut who lives above me. She leaves her TV on all night, and I usually wake up in a sweet LSD-type stupor, dreaming about whoever was on last! Talk about a nightmare!"

After Timmy exits, Ron shakes his head and says to no one, "I've really got to get a real job!"

Timmy's Daewoo pulls up in front of a downtown deli, and his five employees pile out of the car, tripping over each other. As they head toward the door, they look across the street at a large gathering crowd in front of the civic center. The marquee above the center reads "Tonight, Pro Wrestling, 7 p.m."

On the wall outside the center are posters for tonight's show:

New World Wrestling Presents
Live Championship Wrestling
10 exciting matches.
Main Event
Champion Butch Vernon vs. Former Champ J. R. Hotstuff

Timmy's curiosity peaked. He asks, "What's that all about?"

From the group, Tina steps up and says, "Duh! It's only Butch Vernon. He is, like, so hot!"

Wendell agrees with Tina. "You're not kidding. He is so freaking hot!" And then he realizes how that sounds. "I mean hot like he's in everything. Not like I think he's hot!"

Tina elaborates. "He's been in some movies and commercials, and he's got a book coming out soon. And I think he's about to release a Christian CD!"

Timmy shrugs his shoulders. "I've never heard of him. I guess I gotta get out more often."

They all head into the deli. Timmy jumps in front and opens the door. As he enters, he sees a poster for the wrestling show in the deli's window. Dominating the poster is a large color image of Butch Vernon in his wrestling outfit and championship belt. Timmy rubs his chin and wonders if this guy might be vice presidential material.

He looks skyward and says, "I need to know if he's the one, and, if you can help me out, I'd really appreciate it."

Chapter Eighteen

Will You Be My Partner?

The gang from the comedy club was having a great time. Timmy was having a great time. He was as entertaining in this setting as he was onstage. And then he sensed someone staring at him. The guy was in his forties. He was dressed in jeans and a sports coat, and had long hair pulled back into a ponytail.

Finally, the man spoke up. "Hey, Timmy. Timmy Conners. I'm Shaun MacArthur. I used to be a professional wrestler. I'm a big fan. I've been to your club, and I love your work."

Timmy shook his hand. "Are you stalking me? You know they have laws against that."

Shaun laughed. "Believe me, I know!"

Timmy asked, "Do you own this joint?"

"No, no. I work for the New World Wrestling

Organization. I'm in promotions. Like I said, I used to wrestle. But those days are gone thanks to some injuries. We've got a big show across the street tonight. I thought I'd sneak over and grab a bite for me and a couple of my guys."

Timmy shook his head and said, "Yeah, I couldn't help but notice the signs. So, this Butch guy. He's pretty hot right now? At least that's what my crew tells me."

"Yeah, the hottest! Say, would you all like to come to the show tonight? It's sold out, but I've got some passes. I'd love to have you meet Butch later too!"

The kids started jumping up and down with excitement.

"That's pretty nice of you. I guess we could come. Doors open in about an hour, right? Does that include parking?"

Shaun nodded his head. "Of course!" He reached into his coat pocket and pulled out a handful of passes and counted the number of people with Timmy. He handed the passes to Timmy and patted him on the shoulder. "There you go, my man! Front row seats. I'll come get you near the end of the show and take you back to meet the champ."

"Thanks a lot. I look forward to meeting him!"

"You guys enjoy the show! If anyone says anything to you, tell them to see me!"

Timmy decided he needed to go back and type up an agreement for Butch to sign. He told the gang to go ahead, and he'd join them later.

He quickly went back to the office, printed out the agreement, and headed back to the arena. He used his parking pass, made a few rash remarks to the attendant, and headed for the front row—and Sara.

This was his first time at a wrestling show, and he was trying to take it all in. He noticed all the hand-made signs, the t-shirts with wrestler's names on them, and especially the hot-looking girls.

When the matches began, Timmy was amazed at the sound of the wrestlers hitting the ring. He got into the moment and began booing the bad guys and cheering the good guys. It was amazing how fast the night went by. And as things were winding down, just as he said, Shaun showed up and led Timmy's group to the VIP area. All in all, there were about fifty people there.

Timmy had purchased and was wearing a souvenir cap sideways. He also bought a Butch Vernon t-shirt and wore it over his dress shirt. He had drunk a lot of beer and was feeling a little tipsy. He was having a hard time keeping his eyes open—until he saw Meghan, Butch's wife.

Meghan was talking to some promotions people. She looked stunning in a tight dress and high heels. She certainly stood out in the crowd.

Timmy staggered over to her and interrupted her. "Say, weren't you Miss July 2012?" he asked with a bit of a slur. "No, no. I know! You were Miss Casilfornia!"

Meghan and her group moved a couple of feet to the side, hoping Timmy would get the hint. He didn't.

When Meghan tried to walk away, Timmy followed her. "At least tell me you have a thing for older men."

Meghan was about to confront Timmy when the doors opened, and Shaun led Butch into the room.

Butch was wearing an unbuttoned dress shirt and slacks and was still toweling off from his match. The small crowd applauded as the two took a place in the center of the room. When Shaun saw Timmy, he walked Butch over to meet him. But Timmy was starting to fade away, so the former wrestler snapped his fingers in his face to wake him.

"Yo, Timmy. You okay?"

Timmy smiled at Shaun.

"Butch, I want you to meet the champ, Timmy."

Butch steps in front of Timmy, and they are face to chest. Timmy looks Butch up and down and puts his finger on Butch's pecks.

"Are those real? They're ginormous!"

Butch looked toward Shaun. "This is the guy you wanted me to meet?"

Suddenly Timmy remembered why he was there. "Oh,

man, I'm sorry. I must have had one too many tonight! Butch, when you did that thing to that guy, and then he tried to do that other thing back to you . . . that was great!" And then he belched. He looked toward Meghan. "Say, beautiful, I'm not feeling so hot. What's the chance of you taking me home tonight?"

Before Meghan could do or say anything, Butch stepped closer to Timmy.

"I see you've already met my wife!"

Timmy straightened up. "Now I see why she was ignoring me! Butch, I'm sorry! That was a great show tonight. My people just love you!" He pointed to his little crew and their adoring looks. Butch nodded toward them and smiled.

"Say, champ, can I get an autograph? It's for my little cousin. He's not doing so well."

Butch never passed up an autograph request. He grabbed the pen and paper from Timmy and said, "Sure, what's the little fellow's name?"

Timmy pointed at the paper, making sure Butch signs it where he needs him to sign it. "Ah, don't worry about that. He's probably not going to make it anyway. Just sign it right here. He'll be so happy!"

Butch shook his head but signed anyway, anxious to be rid of Timmy. "Okay, here you go. Nice meeting you. Have a nice night. And by the way, nice t-shirt!"

The champ grabbed Meghan and Shaun and turned back to the room, both to mingle and to get away from Timmy.

Timmy waves and says, "Yeah, you too, chump. I mean champ!" He folds the paper and belches again. "Mission accomplished!" he says to no one.

Chapter Nineteen

Read All About It!

Butch had just finished wrestling in front of a sold-out crowd at Madison Square Garden. The promoter found him in the dressing room. Angelo Savage is not only a promoter but the owner of the wrestling company. He's a large, older man, and a former wrestler. He has a tablet under his arm.

Angelo pulled up a chair next to Butch and sat down. When Butch sees him, it's obvious he wasn't as thrilled to see Angelo as Angelo was to see him.

"Butch. Butch. Butch. My main man!"

The champ continued dressing. "Angelo. Angelo. Angelo. You money-grubbing, blood-sucking leach! What do you want?"

Angelo wasn't too thrilled with Butch's greeting. "Have you seen the news lately?"

Butch replied sarcastically, "You have me booked seven

days a week and twice on weekends. When do you think I have any time to watch the news?"

Angelo handed the tablet to Butch. "Then you haven't yet seen this."

The tablet is queued to a news video, and the champ presses the arrow.

"This is Mike Harper reporting for Channel 9 News. Susan, you're not going to believe this. We're outside the Conners for President campaign headquarters, where Tim Conners has just announced that current World Heavyweight Wrestling Champion Butch Vernon will be his running mate for the upcoming presidential campaign..."

Butch raised an eyebrow. "What campaign?"

Angelo shook his head. "Vice president of the Boy Scouts! What the heck do you think? Vice president of the United States of America!"

Butch passes the tablet back to him and nonchalantly resumes dressing.

Angelo's voice raised another octave. "How could you do this to me? Do you know how this is going to mess with my promotions?"

The champ's nerves were a little on edge when he heard Angelo refer to "my promotions." He calmly replied, "I don't know anything about running for vice president, and I thought this was our promotions."

He stood up and reached for his bag. "Anyway, isn't that what you have lawyers for? Send him a letter!"

Butch turned toward the door, but Angelo said, "Wait a minute, Champ. I've rearranged your schedule. I want you in my office at nine tomorrow morning. We're going to get to the bottom of this!"

"Just wait a minute!" Butch said. "I'm working my butt off six to seven days a week. I finally have an opportunity to have a day to myself, and you want me to be in your office first thing in the morning?"

Angelo shook his head. "I didn't commit to run for vice president when I have a contract to wrestle. You made that choice, Mr. Big Man. Now, I've got to get this taken care of. Be in my office tomorrow morning at nine. You got it?"

"I'll be there," Butch relented, "but the rest of the day is mine. Have you got that?"

"I'm just looking out for me and you," Angelo said as he backed away. "I tell you what. I'll buy you and your missus a nice lunch after we get through. Would that make you feel better?"

Butch threw his bag over his shoulder. "Sure thing!" And he stormed toward the door without looking back.

Chapter Twenty

Gifts Come in All Sizes

Butch woke up early and had the coffee going quickly. He was enjoying his first cup when Meghan entered the kitchen. She was beautiful even in a housecoat and slippers.

She kissed Butch and poured herself a cup. "I'm so thrilled you're home for a change. What are we going to do today?"

"Well, I'm sorry," Butch said as he put his cup in the sink, "but I have to meet Angelo this morning. I don't think it will take too long. Why don't we go to lunch at our favorite place afterwards? It'll be Angelo's treat."

"That sounds great! I'll be ready when you get home. Maybe we can go to the bookstore too. I need to get some copies of your book for a couple of friends."

"Don't I have some books in the office?" Butch said as he put his coat on.

"No, you're out. You need to order some more," Meghan said as she hugged him and gave him a kiss. "Hurry back, okay?"

"Oh, you know how much I enjoy my time with Angelo," Butch said sarcastically.

Angelo entered the conference room and put his briefcase on the table. Stephanie, his assistant, was separating papers and placing things before the two lawyers seated at the table.

Angelo looked at the clock. It was 9:07. He shrugged his shoulders.

"Steph, would you please get that Neanderthal on the phone and see where he is?"

She reached for the phone in the middle of the table, but as soon as she did, Butch passed by the conference room window. He was eating an apple as he entered the room.

"Hey, guys. Did I miss anything?" Butch asked.

Angelo was not thrilled. "No, we haven't started yet, but it would be nice if you acted like you cared about what's going on!"

"Well, Angelo, I'm here, and I'm all yours, so let's get started."

Angelo gestured to the two lawyers. "This is Mr. Rolland and Mr. Baker."

Butch left the apple in his mouth, wiped his hand on his T-shirt, and shook hands with them. "Pleased to meet you. Don't get up," he said with a mouthful of apple muffling his words.

Baker handed Butch a piece of paper. "Mr. Vernon, do you recognize this signature?"

Butch picked it up, looked it over, held it up to the light, and then slid it back across the table to the lawyer.

"Yeah, it's my signature. What about it?" Butch said as he threw the apple core into the corner wastebasket.

Rolland picked up the paper and said, "This is your signature on an affidavit that states you agree of your free will to run for vice president of the United States."

Butch reached across and grabbed the paper back. He took a longer look at it this time. Sarcastically he said, "Well, I'll be. Sure looks like it, doesn't it?"

Angelo jumped in. "I, for one, am not happy about this. I want a lawsuit filed by the end of the day. I want to put a stop to this clown act!"

The two lawyers briefly looked at each other. Rolland said, "Hear us out, Angelo, before you make a decision. A lawsuit is very costly, and I know how you don't like to spend money. A lawsuit could run into months or even a year and be very costly."

At the mention of money, they definitely had Angelo's

attention.

Rolland continued, "Our thinking is that we should milk this for all it's worth and run it into some of your story lines. Maybe a setup for a big pay-per-view."

Butch jumped in. "If you're talking about money, I know you have Angelo's attention!"

Angelo rubbed his chin. "I never thought of that. Okay. I'll let this play out for now. But the minute this thing starts to cost me a penny, I'll pull the plug on it! You got it?"

While Rolland and Baker nodded in agreement and began gathering their papers, Angelo added, "And one more thing. I want a face to face with this clown Conners. I want to let him know firsthand who he's dealing with!"

"We can do that!" said Rolland.

After a moment, Butch leaned in and said, "I'm not sure what I'm missing here, but what's this mean for me?"

Angelo answered, "Butch, my friend, for the time being, you are running for the office of the vice president of the United States!"

Butch shook his head. "Oh, great! Like I need one more thing on my plate! So, who's going to validate my parking pass?"

Chapter Twenty-One

Who's in Charge?

The next day Butch was walking through an airport to catch a flight to the next show. When he passed a newsstand, he glimpsed at the magazine rack. He came to an abrupt stop and turned to see if it was really what he thought he saw. His picture on the cover of Time magazine next to a photo of Timmy Conners, with the headline "The New Power Couple."

Next to it was Newsweek with a picture of Timmy in a drunken stupor and a photo of Butch facing him. The headline was "The Third-Party Parties!"

To top it off, The National Inquirer cover has a picture of a shirtless Timmy with his big belly sticking out. A smaller photo in the lower corner shows Butch looking up. The headline reported "Conners Pregnant with Champ's Baby!"

Butch glanced around to see if anyone was looking at him. He picked up a copy of each magazine and placed them under his arm. As he stood in line at the counter, he mumbled under his breath, "The hits just keep on coming!"

Things were more exciting at the Conners campaign office. In its large conference room, seated around a large table, were Timmy, Ron, Angelo, Baker, and Rolland. Timmy and Ron have just finished reading the large legal book presented to them by Angelo and the attorneys. Timmy closed the document and tossed it across the table toward Angelo. The wrestling promoter put up his hand to catch the document before it could slide off the table.

Timmy laughed. "That's pretty funny! You guys should write for the Ledbetter show. I could make that call for you!"

Angelo was not amused. "This isn't a joke. We're very serious about our stipulations, and we expect you to comply fully!"

Timmy reached down and pulled up a handful of magazines. "I especially liked the part where you want me to pay for any lost revenues. Boy, that's not open-ended at all! And you want me to pay a lump sum for current and future licensing? Are you kidding me!?"

He threw the magazines one by one at Angelo.

"Here you go, Angie. Here's Time. Here's Newsweek. Heard of that one? Sports Illustrated. Even Better Homes and Gardens, Men's Fitness, and Playboy. By the way, I want that one back!"

He tossed six more unknown magazines at Angelo. All the magazines had pictures of Butch and Timmy on the front cover. Angelo and the two lawyers' glance at the covers.

"Now let me tell you what I'm gonna do for you!" Timmy said. "What I'm gonna do is foot the bill to keep your golden boy on the cover of every magazine known to man and keep him current in every house from Maine to Hawaii. I'll get him on every daytime talk show, every local news broadcast, and every garbage-can-digging, trash-talking, Kardashian-featuring entertainment news show!"

Timmy hopped up and started marching around the table, making a sound as if he were playing a trombone. "Dah dah dah phrump phrump da ta ta da . . ."

He stopped beside a frustrated Angelo, leaned down, and placed his hands on Angelo's shoulders. "All you have to do is make Butch available to me and make sure he doesn't get a hernia carrying all the bags of cash to the bank!"

Then Timmy resumed his trombone playing. "Bah bah bah dum dum dum du du du . . ."

He returned to his chair and plopped down, out of breath. "Whew! Look, in six months, this will be over, and we can all go back to our lives. I'll go back to telling crappy jokes and chasing women and you guys can go back to exploiting those beasts you call athletes. You dig, Angie?"

Angelo and his lawyers started to pack up their paperwork, defeated.

Timmy answers for Angelo, "Good! Now get out of my office and don't come back unless I invite you back!"

Chapter Twenty-Two

Men in Black

Butch was putting on his boots before a match. Several other wrestlers were getting ready for their own matches, and others were getting dressed in their street clothes, having already wrestled.

Angelo approaches Butch, with two men following close behind. They wear black suits and sunglasses, and no one can miss the little wires that loop over their ears. Everyone stops what they're doing and focuses on the three non-wrestlers.

Butch senses something is up and sees everyone staring in his direction. When he sees Angelo and the men in black, he says, "If these guys are from the IRS, just tell 'em I send my checks in quarterly."

Angelo smiles and shows Butch some papers. "I wish that was all this was. You need to read this."

Butch glances at the papers and every now and then looks toward the two men.

Angelo says, "These guys are going to be with you for a while."

Butch asks, "Is this some new gimmick? You know I don't need any help in the ring. Plus, these guys look a little on the stiff side."

"No, they're not working for me," Angelo says. "They're working for you! Meet Special Agents Fitzpatrick and Simmons. They're assigned to you. They're Secret Service!"

Both agents shake hands with Butch, and Fitzpatrick says, "We'll be part of the team that's assigned to you for the duration of the campaign. But you won't even know we're here."

Butch stands to his feet and towers over the two agents.

"Part of what team? You mean there's more of you guys?" he asks with an eyebrow raised.

"It's all explained in the documents. I suggest you read them thoroughly the first chance you get. This is 24/7 coverage, so we will have a team near you at all times," Simmons explained.

Fitzpatrick added, "But as I said, you won't even know we're around."

Angelo smiled from ear to ear. He leaned in and patted Butch on the shoulder. "You might want to give your wife a call and let her know there's gonna be two more for dinner!"

Suddenly a man opens the door and calls out, "Hey, Champ, you're on in ten minutes!"

Butch looks at Fitzpatrick and Simmons and shakes his head. He grabs his ring coat and belt and heads to the door. "Well, guys, it's ShowTime. I don't know what you're going to do while I'm working, but I'm sure I'll see you after the match."

Butch's match is with the Baron. About ten minutes into the bout Butch whispers to his opponent, "Okay, Nick, throw me out of the ring. Follow me out, and we'll do the chair spot."

The Baron acknowledged, and they did a few more moves, setting up the Baron with the upper hand on Butch. He was ready for the finish. The Baron grabbed Butch and said, "Here we go!"

The Baron arm-whips Butch across the ring, and he flies through the ropes onto the arena floor. The fans aren't too far from where he lands. The Baron jumps out of the ring and onto the floor near Butch. The Baron pushes a man out of his folding chair, folds the chair shut, and lifts it over his head. Butch is staggered from hitting the floor but starting to get to his feet.

Just as the Baron is about to drop the chair onto Butch's head, the two Secret Service agents appear at

Butch's side. They open their coats and show the Baron the stun guns in their holsters. The Baron lowers the chair and slowly hands it to Butch. Butch, trying to stay close to the script, looks at the crowd.

The audience wants Butch to whack the Baron with the chair. So Butch does, sending the Baron to the floor. Butch rolls the Baron into the ring, climbs in behind him—along with the two agents—and covers the Baron as the referee calls out the three-count. The referee grabs Butch's hand and raises it in victory, but both men look quizzically at each other.

"What was that about?" the ref softly asks the champ.

Chapter Twenty-Three

The Debate

For the first time of the many times Timmy has run for president, he is invited to a televised debate, with seven other candidates onstage. The venue is a college campus auditorium, and each candidate stands behind a podium. All the candidates—except Timmy—wear dark suits. Timmy appears instead in a dinner jacket, light-colored slacks, and a western-style tie. He is positioned at the far end of the stage, so far to the end that he is almost offstage. Seated behind a desk at the front of the stage, and facing the candidates, is the moderator, a national news anchor.

About an hour into the debate, the moderator finally addressed Timmy.

"Mr. Conners, would you like to respond to the senator's comments?"

Timmy really hadn't been listening. Instead, he has

been concentrating on a woman in the front row in front of him.

He responds, "What? Huh? Oh, no. I'm sure that old blowhard who's never had a real job or worked a day in his life has made a valid point. But I would like to take this opportunity to ask the future Miss America sitting in the front row if she has any plans after the show?"

The moderator scolded him. "Mr. Conners, this is a very serious forum and all night long you've done nothing but make light of it! If you have no intention of discussing the issues, why do you insist on wasting our time?"

Timmy pointedly answered him. "Are you kidding? This is a serious forum. You bring in a handful of butt-kissing yes-men, throw suits on them, and you think America takes them seriously? Ha! You can open for me at my comedy club with jokes like that!"

The moderator replied, "Mr. Conners, you're out of order! You need to be quiet!"

But Timmy placed his hands in his pockets and stared down the moderator. "That ain't happening, pops. You poked the bear!"

He grabbed the wireless microphone from the podium and walked toward the crowd. "He throws softball questions at these dimwits, and you rubes out there politely applaud every time they finish spewing their B.S.!"

The flustered moderator called out, "Can we get security down here?"

Timmy walks up to one of the other candidates. "Do you remember your answer when you were asked about our troops stationed overseas?"

The candidate looked down at his notes, but Timmy's not waiting for an answer. "Yeah, well, I don't remember what you said either! Blah, blah, blah, and more horse crap! Why can't you be honest and say we want all our troops back home in the States! We've got problems on our borders. Station our troops there! We've got unrest in some of our greatest cities. Station them there! We've got drugs coming in by the boatload—and I mean boatload! Let's station them at our ports! You know, I flew to the Dominican Republic for a comedy show last year. Do you know who greeted me at the airport? The Dominican army! With locked and loaded M16s and MP5s. You want to mess with them?! Good luck! Let me know how that works out for you!"

Some security guards approached Timmy, but when he saw them, he moved into the audience. For their part, most of the crowd is on their feet, standing shocked in disbelief.

Timmy moves toward an exit but doesn't stop talking. "When you ask me a solid question, I'll give you an honest answer! It may not be what you want to hear, not some shined-up turd wrapped in a layer of horse crap, like those dimwits would give you!"

The moderator yelled, "Someone turn off his microphone! Now!"

Timmy turned and made a final appeal to the crowd. "What do you guys think? Am I right, or am I wrong?"

Most of the people cheered and applauded.

Timmy responded, "Darn straight, Skippy! I'm gonna march my patriotic butt right out of these front doors. I will head straight across the street to the nearest bar, and I'll buy everyone in there, plus, everyone in here who comes with me, all the beer they have on tap! Who's with me?"

He dropped the microphone and marched to the door. As he started to exit, some of the crowd followed and then more until only a few people remained in the auditorium.

Chapter Twenty-Four

Can't Touch This!

Butch was in an airport, waiting for a flight to his next show. He used headphones to listen to music while he thumbed through a magazine. He glanced up and noticed people staring at the television in the lounge. Timmy's picture was on the screen, and the chyron headline said, "Candidate loses it at debate!"

After watching for a moment, Butch lowered his head and felt his phone vibrate. The caller ID indicated Angelo was calling. He decided not to take the call.

Meanwhile, Ron walked into Timmy's office and found the candidate preparing to eat his lunch.

"What the heck, man!" Ron nearly shouted as he threw the newspaper on the desk, covering Timmy's sandwich.

"Hey, watch it!" Timmy said and glanced at the paper. "Yeah, uh-huh. Not a very good picture of me! I look old!"

"Tim, what were you thinking?" Ron asked. "Were you stoned or something?"

Timmy reaches for the remote and clicks on the television. It's tuned to a news channel, and the talking heads are yammering on and on about Timmy's performance at the debate. The candidate switches to another news channel. A panel of journalists is mewling about Timmy's perceived meltdown. He changes to another news channel, which is running footage of Timmy's harangue at the debate. He pushes the mute button and picks up his sandwich.

Ron flops into a chair. "So, this was planned? Going for publicity?"

"I wouldn't say planned," Timmy answered. "But that little wormy a-hole got under my skin. So I figured, 'What the heck! What do I have to lose?' Now, not only are we getting headlines in every newspaper from coast to coast, but we're also leading every news show."

A couple of days later Butch was leaving his gym after a hard workout. He wore sweatpants and a sleeveless T-shirt. As he approached his car, he saw a national news reporter and a cameraman rush toward him.

"Excuse me, Mr. Vernon. Teddy Brown with SE1 News. May we ask you a few questions?"

Butch had never been shy around the media, and he

stopped, smiled into the camera, and said, "Sure. I can give you a few minutes. What do you got?"

"Would you comment on Tim Conners' erratic behavior at last night's debate?"

"Erratic!" Butch repeated. "You haven't spent much time around him, have you? He's a free spirit and sometimes, well, most of the time, he says what's on his mind. For the most part, I find that refreshing. Then again there's times when I feel like dropping him with a power slam!"

Brown followed up with a political question. "What are your thoughts on Mr. Nelson's attempts to force the hand of the World Agricultural Council on restricting the trade of overseas produce?"

The wrestler looked at the reporter and smiled at the attempted gotcha question.

"Good question, Teddy. That's the kind of question where you'd think an athlete wouldn't have any idea what you're talking about. But I believe Prime Minister Nelson's speculation that higher taxation on certain imported agricultural products will affect the market as it pertains to commonly traded natural reserves. But he's not taking into account the excess of unused trade goods. So, his plan looks good on paper, but it won't hold water in the real world."

The stunned reporter stood frozen in his tracks for a

moment, not expecting an answer, much less a detailed answer, like that from Butch. "Um, ah, um, I, ah. Thank you."

Butch replied, "Anytime. Have a good one." And he turned back toward his car, then he stopped and turned to the reporter.

"By the way, Teddy," he said, "I'll take Tim Conners' honesty about what's going on in the country more to heart than the crap that is coming from the dinosaurs who have made politics a lifetime occupation. Tim's doing pretty well with his comedy club. He doesn't need to be running for office. Sure, he's getting lots of publicity, but the reason he's getting publicity is because the American people are finally seeing through what the politicians have been doing for decades. Tim is becoming America's choice for president. He's an outsider, and Washington, New York, and Los Angeles frankly don't like it!"

The reporter seemed speechless, so Butch waved and walked away. "See ya around, Teddy!"

Chapter Twenty-Five

Let's Get Ready to Rumble

Butch and Meghan met Timmy and Ron for lunch. While Butch and Meghan ordered healthy meals—salads and fish—and Ron ordered something light, Timmy ordered his customary steak and fries.

"I hate to admit it," Ron started the conversation, "but Tim's rant the other night seems to have paid off."

Timmy added, "I told you it would!"

"Tim has been invited to next week's debate in Minnesota," Ron told Butch and Meghan. "This is the big one. All the front-runners will be there. We really appreciate you two making time for us."

Butch and Meghan nodded over their salads.

"The reason we wanted to talk to you, that is, you two," Ron resumed, "is that we want to include you in this. We want you both to be there, and we'd like you to spend some time with Tim before the debate."

Butch put his fork down and looked at the campaign manager. Tim smiled before his next bite of steak. Butch lifted his fork and then put it down and looked at Timmy. The candidate had steak sauce on his chin and a couple of ketchup-covered fries on his fork. Butch looked back at Ron and said, "What exactly is it you think you'll accomplish by having me spend time with him?"

Ron explained, "You're an athlete. It's obvious you've trained hard to get where you are and look how you look—"

He looked at Timmy, who appears to be having gas pains.

Ron resumed, "Tim's never trained for anything a day in his life. Now I'm not talking about you training him to be an athlete. Those days passed for Tim a long time ago. But I'm talking about you training him for this debate."

Butch rocked back in his seat and looked at Meghan.

"Look, Butch," Ron said, "I've seen the way you handle yourself. Sometimes you don't know what you're talking about, but you always say it with confidence and assurance. I need you to work with Tim to try and get that same feeling out of him. Plus, you're the only one big enough to keep him sober until then."

Timmy nodded his head at that and then turned his

attention to a nearby table of young women. The girls all smiled back at him.

Butch said, "You know you're asking the impossible. But I'll give it a shot. You need to get with Angelo and clear my schedule. Have Timmy at my place tomorrow morning at eight."

Surprised that Butch would agree so easily, Ron cocked his head to one side. "Ah, I'll tell him eight, but if I were you, I'd expect him more around nine. He's not really a morning person."

They all looked at Timmy again and went back to eating their dinner.

The next morning, Butch and Timmy go over some newspaper articles from a stack of papers a foot high on the table. Butch points out an article, but Timmy focuses on the comics on the next page.

Butch turns on the television and switches to a news channel. After a few minutes he changes it to another news channel. Timmy reaches for the remote and tunes in to a rerun of Three's Company. "That Suzanne Somers was hot, right?"

Butch takes back the remote and returns to the news. After getting a feel for what all the news shows were talking about, the two turned to their laptops. They both use earphones, and Butch is taking notes on a pad. He's writing down stats and sketching some charts and graphs. When he glances at Timmy's laptop, he sees that Timmy has gone to YouTube and found a video of a bikini contest.

They take a break, and Meghan joins them to shop for some new clothes for Timmy. After looking over a few things, Timmy holds up a white maître d' suit, but both Butch and Meghan shake their heads no. Butch holds up a navy-blue suit and light blue dress shirt. Timmy shakes his head no. But Butch and Meghan overrule him.

It was a long day for all of them. At the end of the day Timmy is exhausted and splayed out on a couch. Butch is going over his notes. After a while, Butch looked over and saw that Timmy was sound asleep with a plate of food on his chest. The wrestler quietly picked up the uneaten meal, turned off the light, and walked out. Before he leaves the room, he turns, looks at Timmy, covers him with a blanket, smiles, and walks out.

Chapter Twenty-Six

The Second Debate

Debate night came quickly. Butch, Meghan, Ron, and Timmy were backstage with dozens of well-dressed people. Timmy's heart rate was pretty high as he anticipated what was going to happen onstage before the nation tonight. A gray-haired man wearing a thousand-dollar suit passed, and Timmy and his small entourage recognized the front-runner, Martin Pounders. They paused to watch him walk by and noted how smooth he was around the people clustered here.

As soon as the distinguished candidate was out of earshot, Ron said, "That's Pounders! Holy smokes! This is the big time, Timmy!"

Butch commented, "Nice suit."

Timmy simply shrugged. "I agree. That's a good-looking man. If I was gonna go homo, that'd be the one!"

The manager and the wrestler look at each other and shake their heads.

Timmy continues, "I'm just saying, you know, like if zombies were gonna eat my brains unless I made it with a guy, well, he'd be at the top of the list! But I'm not saying there's a list or anything." Under his breath he mumbles, "Brad Pitt, George Clooney, Mario Lopez..."

Butch grabbed Timmy's lapels and pulled him close. "Okay, get your mind right! You're ready for this! Don't back down! Show them who you are! Now, go out there and get 'em!"

The wrestler turns Timmy around and slaps his butt. Timmy decides to react as if he has just been goosed. He gives them a thumbs-up and walks onstage.

Ron shakes his head. "They're gonna chew him up and spit him out!"

"Oh, yeah. He doesn't stand a chance!" Butch agreed.

Again, Timmy found himself with seven other candidates on stage. All of them stood behind identical podiums. The comedian noted seven white men and one African American, the latter at the far end of the stage, symmetrical to Timmy, who stood stage left. Television cameras flanked the stage, and Secret Service agents seemed to be everywhere. Seated at a desk at the front of the stage, with his back to the audience, was national news anchor Gerald Douglas, the evening's moderator.

After pitching several questions to the candidates, Douglas addresses Timmy. "Mr. Conners, a lot has been said about your lengthy arrest record. Would you like to say anything about that to the American people tonight?"

Timmy looks uncomfortable. Not only was he not used to standing in the same spot for such a long time, but he's starting to feel uncomfortable in his formal suit.

He searches for words and then responds, "Oh, wow, you're finally gonna get me involved. Wow, man, is it hot up here or is it just me?"

The moderator seems actually concerned for the candidate on the hot seat. "Mr. Conners, if you'd feel more comfortable, please loosen your tie."

Timmy glanced offstage at Butch. "Sorry, Butch. I don't see how you guys can spend all day in these monkey suits!"

He leaned toward the podium and looked at the other candidates but addressed his words to the candidate at the end of the line. "No offense, Mr. Jackson. How you doing down there, brother? Look, if they ask you to bus these tables after this shindig, I'll give you a hand. We're not afraid of the Man!"

Gerald Douglas interrupted Timmy's riff. "Mr. Conners, please refrain from turning this debate into a routine for your comedy club."

Timmy riveted his eyes on the moderator. "Sorry, your honor. Okay, back to your question. Yes, I've been arrested numerous times, mostly D&D—that's drunk and disorderly to you lay people. No big deal. I had a little drinking problem. I'm kinda like Otis from the old Andy Griffith Show. They'd give me the key to a cell, and I came and went as I pleased!"

The moderator interrupted. "Well, you can make light of your drinking problem, but I doubt the American public would want a drunk in the White House!"

Timmy smirked. "You mean, like, again? The last one didn't do so bad!"

Before the moderator can say anything, Timmy instinctively turns the tables. "Say, you know, I've been standing here and listening to you lob softball questions to the guys up here. And I'd like to ask my fellow candidates a question or two."

The moderator responded, "That's not how these things operate. We need to follow the guidelines all the parties agreed to before—."

But Timmy interrupted him. "Follow, smollow! Let's ask the two big wheels in the middle, since they seem to be the chosen front-runners!" He turned to face Martin Pounders and Donald Hampton who were center stage.

Pounders said, "It can't hurt to see what the fellow has

to say. I'm willing!" And Hampton added, "I can only imagine what thoughts are rolling around in his head. Let him ask his questions."

The audience applauded, startling the moderator.

Timmy began. "Mr. Hampton, do you know what the average American's take-home pay is?"

Hampton responded, "That is an interesting question. America is a diverse and divided nation. To pinpoint one's take-home pay would be difficult as there are many factors, such as age, race, and nationality..."

Timmy interrupted him. "That's crap, man! Let me ask you again, do you know what the average Joe in America brings home or not?"

The audience erupted with applause and cheers, which startled Hampton. He tried to answer, "Well, don't hold me to this figure, but I would say fifty to sixty thousand dollars a year!"

Timmy pounced quickly. "Hello? Is anyone there? Try twenty-eight thousand dollars. Actually, twenty-eight thousand and five hundred dollars. Man, you are way off!" He paused long enough to take a breath. "Mr. Pounders, can you tell us how many properties you and your wife own?"

Pounders was surprised at the question. "The right to own property," he said, "is one of the greatest rights we, as

Americans, have. When our forefathers came over to this great country, they envisioned a land where everyone was free to purchase the ground under his feet as a place to call home. They…"

Timmy interrupted. "Hey, man! Do you know or not? Simple question, bub!"

Pounders answered, "I, ah, believe my wife and I own a total of five properties."

Timmy turned to the audience and smiled. "You know, there's this Google thing out there, pal. It lets anyone with a keyboard see who owns what. And when I googled it, I saw that you and your wife own nine properties, and they're worth about fifty million dollars all together! Wow! Good for you! I hope you can find those four missing houses!"

As Pounders tries to respond, the crowd begins to boo him.

Finally the candidate says, "I can explain that discrepancy. Some of those properties are being held in trust—." And then the boos drown him out.

The moderator interrupts Timmy's attack. "We'll be right back after this short break!"

The crowd, however, was energized, and the Secret Service agents who were scattered across the auditorium received orders to be ready for anything.

When the debate resumed, the moderator said, "We apologize for that break in protocol. Our next question is for Mr. Zane. Senator Zane, what are your thoughts on protecting the border?"

As the senator answered the question, it felt as if all the oxygen had been sucked out of the room by Timmy. The rest of the night was uneventful. Timmy was the only candidate who made the night worth watching. Afterward, the pundits all agreed it had been a very successful night for the comedian.

Chapter Twenty-Seven

We're Moving on Up!

A couple of days later, at the Conners campaign headquarters, Timmy was seated at a large table, surrounded by a group of staffers and volunteers. The candidate looked tired. And he was uncharacteristically quiet.

Ron entered, waving a newspaper over his head. "I've got some great news. USA Today published its exit poll. As we expected, Pounders and Hampton are in a dead heat at forty percent of the vote. But the big news for us is that Tim comes in at an amazing eleven percent!"

The staffers and volunteers cheered the news, and one of them slapped Timmy's shoulder. It woke him up.

"Timmy, did you just hear what I said?" Ron asked.

"What's all that mean?" Timmy asked. "I'm not very good with numbers."

"It means a couple of things. You've never had more than three percent of any straw poll. This is a big turn for us. It makes you a credible candidate!"

Before that could sink in for Timmy, another staffer burst into the room and ran toward Ron. "Mr. Hillman, there's something you need to see."

Ron grabbed the television remote, but Timmy jumped out of his chair and flung himself toward the remote. Ron had already pressed the power button and the flat screen filled with swim suited contestants in the Miss World Teeny Bikini Contest. Everyone—that is, mostly the women—immediately looked at Timmy.

"The darn cable company!" he said. "They keep mixing my signals and this kind of stuff keeps popping up! I'm gonna call them first thing tomorrow!"

"Tim, that was a pay-per-view channel," Ron said. "You had to order it!"

"Weird, right?" Timmy shrugged.

Ron turned to a news channel in time to hear a reporter say, "It was revealed early this morning that a former aide of Senator Martin Pounders has come forward with allegations of sexual misconduct. The young woman's identity is being withheld for her protection. The senator's camp has made no comment. We will keep you posted on events as they happen. Back to you..."

Ron was elated. "Tim, you know what this means, right?"

Timmy's voice was nervous. "Does it mean they are gonna talk to all the girls that have worked for me?"

"No, Tim. It means that his forty percent of the vote is going to take a nosedive. And all of those voters are going to need someone to follow. Someone they can relate to."

"You mean the black guy?" Timmy guessed. "He seems like a cool cat. I'd hang out with him!"

"No, no, no. I'm thinking more along the line that they might support you!"

A moment later Timmy understood. "Oh, yeah. The worse he looks, the better I look. Kinda like when you drop a steamer in a public john, but then some three-hundred-pound Pakistani two stalls down craps out a baby elephant. Yours don't smell so bad anymore!"

He seemed proud of his analogy, but Ron and the rest of the group shook their heads.

Ron tries to pull Timmy to the side, even though Timmy tries to fight him. "Timmy, I wasn't going to tell you this, but I guess now is as good...or bad, a time as any." Timmy looks around, already confused by what is going on. "Okay, spit it out, old boy! Well, don't spit it out, what a stupid expression! What if I was eating the best piece of steak I've ever eaten? You come along and say, 'spit it out'!

I don't think so, mister!"

Ron is actually lost in Timmy's rant, but he tries to get them back on track. "Whatever! Look, the Libertarian Party wants to nominate you as their candidate for this election! Do you know what that means?"

Obviously, Timmy has no idea what Ron is talking about but Timmy tries his best to bluff his way through the conversation. "Look, the only way I'd have anything to do with a Library Party is if there was one of those sexy librarians! You know, with glasses and her hair up in a bun. She'd pull out a ruler and threaten to spank me if I didn't stop passing gas in the reading room!"

Ron just had a blank look on his face.

Timmy continues his fantasy. "She would let her long hair down and shake her head. Then she'd take her glasses off and look at me real seductive like!"

Timmy stops and turns to Ron. "Can you make that happen? I'd join that party if she was there!"

Ron puts his hand on Timmy's shoulder and starts to lead him out into the common area. Ron is shaking his head as they walk. "Sure thing champ, I'll get right to work on that librarian for you!"

Timmy and Ron enter a common area where a handful of volunteers are still working. They approach a young African American man.

"Tim, we're going to have Carlton here drive you home. You know, you don't look too good. You need to get some sleep. The rest of us have got a lot of work to do."

Young Carlton smiles at Timmy, and Timmy slowly joins him. Everyone in the room, especially those who had spent time with Timmy, noticed he was moving slowly and seemed to be out of breath.

"Not a bad idea," Timmy said. "I've been feeling kinda funny the last couple of weeks."

He looked at Carlton. "Hey, wanna swing by Uncle Phil's and see if there's anything in the fridge?"

Carlton didn't get the Fresh Prince reference, but he humored Timmy with a chuckle. "Ah, no sir. I think we should just get you home."

Within seconds of Carlton getting him in the car, Timmy was sound asleep.

Chapter Twenty-Eight

Hopefully Dreams Don't Come True

As Timmy approached his comedy club and campaign headquarters, he saw a large crowd in front, so he diverted to the back parking area and nervously wondered what all those people were doing out front. "Darn, it finally happened!" he said. "That CD I sent out. They must have figured out I just renamed an old one and want their money back!"

He reached in the back seat and found a towel. After draping it over his head, he looked around anxiously to see if anyone was watching. When he believed the coast was clear, he got out of his car and used the service entrance.

When he passed the conference room, he saw it was full of staffers and Ron. As soon as he stepped in, everyone quieted down. Timmy dropped his towel on a chair and walked toward Ron.

"Morning, Tim. Are you all right?" the campaign manager asked.

Taking a deep breath, Timmy said, "I don't know what's going on out there, but if all those people want refunds, I'm gonna need to file a chapter whatever!"

Ron laughed. "They don't want any money back! They're here to volunteer for the campaign! Tim, they're all here to help you. Heck, the phones have been ringing off the hook with people wanting to be on your team!"

After breathing a sigh of relief, Timmy said, "Are you saying I don't have to pay them anything? Just one T-shirt each? I'd better check eBay".

"We've got it, Tim! Why don't you go out front and shake some hands? Give them a pep talk, thank them for coming. Tell them how much you appreciate them joining the team."

A few moments later Timmy was working the crowd like a professional. The volunteers loved it and said how eager they were to work for the 'Conners for President' campaign.

The next night Timmy, his wife and ex-wives and children and stepchildren were all on stage. The convention center was packed to the rafters with people excited to be there.

Timmy was dressed in a tacky red-white-and-blue suit. He waved to the crowd from the stage, walking from one end to the other and occasionally pointing to certain people and making eye contact. A band played amid a shower of confetti and balloons.

Butch and Meghan were also onstage. When they saw how Timmy dressed, they smiled at each other and shook their heads. When Timmy looked their way, Butch gave him a thumbs-up.

At a certain point the band concluded its concert, and Timmy walked to the podium. Amid the crowd's cheers, he said, "Thank you. Thank you. Thank you, ladies and gentlemen. I want you to know I'm going to be the best darn president you've ever had!"

The cacophony resumed and the room filled with miniature flags, as everyone waved them and called out their support.

Timmy backed away from the podium, and a bearded man dressed in olive drab military surplus gear ran past Butch. The man produced a handgun and yelled something unintelligible. The sound of shots reverberated throughout the auditorium. Butch saw Timmy thrown off his feet by the impact of the bullets striking his chest. Timmy's arms were outstretched as he fell backward.

Butch saw it all, but his body was frozen in place. Suddenly the action slowed, as if his mind needed to process the scene into something resembling reality.

After the fourth shot, Butch saw Timmy roll toward him and look him in the eye. And then his head fell to the stage as a line of blood leaked from his mouth.

Still watching events unfold in slow motion, Butch saw the assassin turn toward him, the man's face contorted with rage, his eyes wild. He swung his gun hand toward Butch, and said, "You're next, Mr. Vice President!"

Butch bolted upright in bed from the nightmare and yelled, "No!"

Meghan woke up, "What is it, baby! Who are you yelling at?"

Butch decided he couldn't tell her about the nightmare, so he said, "Just a bad dream. Don't worry about it. Go on back to sleep."

But he couldn't go back to sleep. So, he got up and grabbed a glass from the kitchen. A few moments later he sat in the living room in the dark, pondering the nightmare. It seemed so real.

The next morning, Butch got dressed and told Meghan he had to see Timmy and Ron. He drove like a madman to campaign headquarters. He saw the parking lot was full of people. Some were there to volunteer, but most were there just to catch a glimpse of Timmy or Butch.

After he'd parked his car and opened the door, he was surrounded by a crowd of camera phones. People called out, "Hey, champ! We're pulling for you guys!"

Normally Butch would have mingled with the crowd for a while, but he was determined to find Ron and Timmy. He quickly made his way straight into the conference room.

Butch saw Timmy draped over a chair, engrossed in a magazine. The wrestler smiled and thought it was the first time he had seen Timmy read anything. He wondered if Timmy had finally discovered that Time and Newsweek had something to them other than covers. And then he had a better view. Mad magazine.

Timmy looked up. "Wow, partner, you look as if you ran to get here. Take a seat. Catch your breath. You look worn out."

Ron looked up from the other side of the room. He, too, saw that Butch was almost out of breath.

Both men got up and approached Butch.

Butch looked at them and said, "I had a crazy dream last night. We won the election."

Timmy smiled. "Hey, I like this dream!"

And then Butch told him about the worst of it. "As soon as you started to say something onstage, some nut job raced up and shot you!"

"Huh? What?" Timmy said.

"And then he pointed the gun at me!" Butch said, and took a second to catch his breath. "This is starting to worry me. Everywhere I go, I see our faces. Every radio station, every TV program. It's starting to get to me!"

Timmy placed a hand on Butch's shoulder. "Buddy, I think you need to back off those horse pills you're taking. Look, I gotta tell you, we've been climbing in the polls. Now, I'm not saying we have a snowball's chance of winning. But I'm saying we have a chance! Maybe for the next couple of weeks, you and I need to stay close to each other."

Timmy held up his hand with two fingers close together. "You know, like two pills and some pot!'

"Don't you mean two peas in a pod?" Butch said.

Timmy shook his head. "No. No. It's two pills and some pot! You know, like, you get a couple of pills, you put 'em in a small pill case, and then you jam some weed in there. You know, for emergencies! Ta-da! Two pills and some pot!"

Ron leaned toward Butch. "Just go with it. Humor him."

"Yup," the champ said. "You and me. Two pills and some pot. That's us!"

Ron nodded. "I'm going to get out there with the volunteers. We've got a whole new crew we're training. Why don't you two spend some time together? Might be good for both of you."

Timmy agreed and then turned toward Butch. "Yeah, why don't you fill me in on what you've been up to? Maybe later we can go down the street and get some chink food for lunch! You people eat Chinese, right?"

Butch cocked his head to one side. "What do you mean by you people?"

"Well, um, athletes," Timmy said. "I didn't know if you athletes could eat that crap. Lord knows, there's no telling what it's doing to my insides. They say an hour after you eat Chinese, you're hungry again. With me it's more like ten minutes after. It makes me crap my guts out, but it sure tastes good going down."

Timmy picked up his Mad magazine and pointed something out to Butch. "Now, that's funny!"

Chapter Twenty-Nine

Breaking News

Nothing like this had ever happened to one of Timmy's campaigns, but then this campaign was unlike any he had run before. So many things were happening, it was getting harder and harder for Ron to actually sleep. He couldn't go an hour without checking the national news. He devoured newspapers and magazines and listened to every podcast that had anything to say about the election.

Tonight's evening news programs had stirred him up. He was still awake at 2:18 a.m. and he didn't even have a thought about going to bed. Sleep, however, was no problem for Timmy. Whenever he went to bed, he fell fast asleep. This was aided greatly by his CPAP machine, which had been a great help to him ever since his doctor had diagnosed sleep apnea as his problem.

Unfortunately, Timmy had never learned to use the do-not-disturb feature on his phone, and when Ron called, the candidate nearly jumped out of bed. Timmy ripped off his air mask and mumbled into the phone, "Yeah, yeah. Did her water break?"

When the fog began to lift from his brain and he realized he was talking to Ron, he said, "What's up? Did they find another body in the freezer?"

"No, Tim. No. Can you turn on a TV and not get distracted with another bikini contest?"

"Yeah, yeah, yeah. Give me a minute."

Timmy reached for a remote and sat at the foot of the bed. "Okay. What am I looking for?"

"Turn it to SE1?" Ron said. "There's a breaking story about Hampton!"

Timmy found the news channel and saw a B-level anchor transposed in front of an unflattering photo of Democratic front-runner Donald Hampton. The caption read "Racial slurs leaked."

The anchor summarized, "Our breaking news tonight is the release of a video of Democratic candidate Donald Hampton unleashing a torrent of racial slurs at a private fundraiser. The candidate was apparently unaware his comments were being recorded. We must warn viewers, even though we have edited the audio for broadcast, some viewers may find the video to be shocking and offensive."

The screen filled with a camera-phone video that showed the candidate in front of a small group of people in a private home. Hampton's distinctive voice said, "I'm telling you, if I ever catch that bleep anywhere near my wine cellar again, I'm going to take him out back and whip him like my grandpappy used to whip his bleep! Bleep, bleep bleep of a bleep!"

When the anchor returned, he said, "SE1 has reached out to Mr. Hampton's campaign for comment, but we've had no response. Stay tuned to SE1 for further developments."

"Wow!" Timmy said. "I can't believe it!"

"I know," Ron said.

"That sucker has a wine cellar!" Timmy went on. "And I thought I was living large with that two pack of chardonnay we picked up at Sam's the other day."

When Ron didn't answer, Timmy asked, "Dang, Ron, you still there?"

Rubbing his forehead in frustration, Ron said, "Still here. Tim, do me a favor. Don't say anything to anyone and come straight here in the morning. In fact, just ask the Secret Service agents to bring you here and we'll talk then, okay?"

"Sure thing, bud. Okay if I go back to sleep now?" Timmy said.

"Sure, you can, Tim," Ron said. "Sweet dreams. See you in a few hours."

Chapter Thirty

And the Winner Is . . .

On Election Day morning Butch and Meghan were in the midst of their workout. They always worked out together whenever Butch wasn't on the road. Their attention was on the news, though.

"We're going to throw it to Erik, who is reporting from an eastern voting precinct. Erik, how's the turnout so far?" the anchor asked.

Erik was Asian American and dressed in a dark suit. He was positioned in front of a polling place.

"Thanks, Martin," he said. "The turnout so far has been sparse, but it's still early. This is a working-class neighborhood. What we might call middle America."

Martin asked, "Have you been able to get a feel for how the early voting is going so far?"

With a pleasantly surprised look on his face, Erik

responded, "Yes, I have, and believe it or not, Libertarian candidate Timothy P. Conners by far seems to be getting the most support. At least, that's what I'm hearing from the people who are answering our exit poll, as you'll see in my recent conversations with a few voters."

In the video that followed, an older man said, "I voted for that Conners fella. You know, he's the only one the missus and me trust. All them other idiots are crooks anyway!"

This was followed by an interview with a young mother with three children, "Are you kidding me?" she asked. "These boys wouldn't let me vote for anyone other than Butch. At our house it's Butch Vernon dolls, Butch Vernon action figures. Why Sam here almost broke Joe's arm the other day doing some kind of wrasslin' hold he saw Butch do. No, no. I didn't have any choice but to vote for the wrestler and that comedian."

Erik returned in front of the camera, smiling and slightly shaking his head. "Reporting from Bucks County, this is Erik Tran."

The national anchor summarized, "This seems to be an interesting trend, at least from our early reports. Stay tuned to SE1 for the latest on the election results. Our national coverage begins tonight at 7:00 p.m. eastern standard time, 8:00 p.m. central."

Butch paused his workout, wiped his face with a towel, and glanced at Meghan. Both of them smiled.

Later, Butch and Meghan went out for lunch at a nearby sports bar and grill. Whenever other diners passed by, they gave Butch a thumbs-up. The walls were covered with large flat screens, but they were not tuned into any of the sports channels. Everyone, instead, was on a news channel offering wall-to-wall election coverage.

Butch glanced up at the closest screen and flagged down the first server he saw. He pointed to the television. "Hey, partner, can you turn that up?"

"Yes sir, Mr. Vernon!" said the server, ecstatic to be called on by the champ.

A moment later everyone around Meghan and Butch heard, "We're going to Kelly Quintos, who is standing by in Libertarian candidate Tim Conners' hometown. Kelly, have you received any word on Mr. Conners' whereabouts this afternoon?"

"Yes, Gloria," the reporter said, "we have word that Mr. Conners is actually voting as we speak. I've talked to some other voters as they have been exiting from the polling station. And there is no doubt the people here are voting in droves to support their local boy."

A clip of a young woman responding to the reporter's

question fills the screen. "Yes, we voted for our Timmy. He's the only one in that group we trust!"

Another said, "Unfortunately, with the state of the economy, our government's reluctance to pull our troops out of foreign countries, and the horrible shape of our own infrastructure, the Congress has made this country a joke. If I have to laugh, I want a comedian in the White House. So, I voted for Conners and Vernon!"

The field reporter resumed her description of the activity around the polling place. "Gloria, I'm getting word that Mr. Conners has left the polling precinct, and he's being followed by a small army of neighbors and supporters, all cheering him on. He's headed our way. I'm going to see if I can get a word with him."

When the reporter and her cameraman approach Timmy, he's smiling from ear to ear. Kelly said to him, "Congratulations, Mr. Conners. So far, the people we've talked to have indicated they're supporting you en masse in this election. Do you think this is just hometown support, or is it an indication of your chances across the country today?"

"How do I feel about my chances today?" Timmy repeated. "Well, I feel bleeping great! Does this country rock or what?" And the small crowd around him cheered and waved little flags and showed off their Conners for

President T-shirts.

Fortunately, the studio had caught Timmy's unconventional language before it hit the airwaves.

The reporter resumed, "Yes, yes, it sounds like your supporters agree with you. Can you tell us what your plans are for the rest of the day?"

"Well, from here," Timmy answered, "we're all taking a bus to the Cornerstone Senior Center off State Road 14 to visit with the people there, and then we're heading to a soup kitchen to serve some of the homeless. And later this afternoon we're going downtown for a pep rally for gay and lesbian rights—" He paused, sweat pouring from his brow, and laughed.

"Nah, I'm just pulling your chain. We're taking a bus all right, but it's heading to Hooters! The hot wings and beer are on me today!"

The crowd around Timmy went wild. The candidate turned back to the reporter. "If you want to come along, there's always room on my lap for one more!"

And he turned and marched the small entourage toward a large bus.

Kelly realized her mouth was agape when the camera returned to her. "Reporting from the Conners campaign, I'm Kelly Quintos."

Butch looked for the server. "Any chance you can find

some golf or tennis maybe?" "Sure thing Champ!" said the server. Butch shook his head and continued eating.

Chapter Thirty-One

Holy Smokes!

The convention center was packed and buzzing. Onstage was a huge Imax screen. Off to the side a band played background music.

A large map of the United States fills the Imax screen. Some of the Eastern States are red for the Republican candidate, some are blue for the Democrat candidate, but most of them are green, for Timmy Conners. Many of the western states are white. It's almost 11:00 p.m. EST.

At the bottom of screen is a voter tally by color of the party:

Hampton/Childs—38,495,169
Pounders/Banks—36,141,238
Conners/Vernon—48,615,442

The image of a news commentator suddenly filled the screen.

"Good evening, America! I'm Phillip Sanders with this election update. We are getting more polling results from some of our West Coast affiliates. Let's go to Hannah Sayers and see what they're reporting."

The map that fills the screen is similar to the one that had been onscreen prior to the update, and Hannah announces the latest figures. When the camera returns to the small panel of four news commentators, all have looks of surprise. Sanders takes off his glasses and rubs his chin. He then takes another look at the monitor on his desk.

"This must be a mistake. This is unofficial—and unbelievable—but with a majority of the polling precincts and states reporting in, it appears that Libertarian candidate Timothy P. Conners is the next president of the United States!"

The anchor turned to someone off camera. "This can't be right. We need to recheck all these numbers!"

The Connors campaign people are jammed into the green room at the convention center. As soon as Timmy hears the words "Conners is the next president," Timmy starts to chug a beer. When he finishes, with beer running down the sides of his mouth, he shouts, "Yes! Yes! Yes! I am the champ! Let's see one of you losers beat that!"

Suddenly the door to the room burst open, and Ron and a handful of aides' head straight toward Timmy.

Ron grabbed Timmy by the shoulders, smiling ear to ear. "Tim! Tim! You're not going to believe this! ABC, CBS, NBC, SE1, Fox, and Newsmax are all calling it! For us! The only holdouts are CNN and MSNBC."

Timmy wiped the beer from his face and stared at Ron.

"Come again? All these guys are calling me? Well, give me the phone. I want to talk to them. Maybe some of 'em can bring some pizza."

"No, no, Tim," Ron said. "They're not calling you. They're calling the election! They're calling it for you! They're saying you won!"

But Timmy doesn't react.

Ron takes charge, pushing Timmy toward an aide. "Get him cleaned up. Where's his family? Get them ready. Who's got his speech?"

Chapter Thirty-Two

Hail to the Chief!

Timmy and his family, Butch and Meghan, Ron, some aides, and about twenty friends make their way to the stage as the band plays "Hail to the Chief!"

Timmy fights through the balloons and confetti streaming down onstage as he staggers to the podium. Behind him a screen is filled with the exclamation "Conners Wins!" and the latest vote tally. Ron reminds Timmy to watch the teleprompter, gives him a hug, and wishes him good luck.

The victorious candidate steps to the podium and says, "Well, what the heck do you think of this, folks?"

The crowd responds with cheers.

"Truthfully, I didn't see this coming!" Timmy says. "Now I'm kinda sorry I've been drinking all day!"

Again, the crowd cheers.

Timmy turns back and gestures for Butch to join him. "Butch. Champ! Come on over here, man!"

Butch smiles and waves to the acclamation of the crowd as he steps up beside Timmy at the podium.

"Before I say anything else, I want you to give it up for one of the greatest guys I know. My running mate and the world heavyweight wrestling champion, Mr. Butch Vernon!"

The swell of the crowd's cheering is deafening. Caught up in the moment, Timmy throws his arms around Butch. But that only accentuates the difference in the physical presence of the men, with the wrestler standing more than a head taller than the comedian.

Suddenly Timmy's breathing becomes labored, and he feels some numbness in one of his arms. He turns back to the podium and tries to steady himself by gripping it with both hands.

"Wow!" he says. "I don't think there's any way I could lift Butch up more than he's lifted me over these past four months. Plus, confidentially, he's a lot heavier than I thought. I'd definitely need a crane!"

The crowd responds with laughs and cheers, but Ron and Butch note that Timmy slurs the last few words.

Timmy has trouble breathing and begins to sway.

"I, I have a speech here, somewhere," he says and then

looks back at Butch and Ron. "I'm not, not feeling . . . too good, guys." And he drops to the floor of the stage. The thud echoes through the cavernous hall.

Butch runs over and opens Timmy's shirt collar. Immediately a squad of EMTs appear, surrounding Timmy and pushing Butch out of the way. They start CPR on Timmy as a cordon of security people and Secret Service agents form a physical shield around the fallen figure. Secret Service agents swarm around Butch and Meghan, escorting them off stage and into a safe room.

A few moments later Timmy is on a gurney and being rushed into an ambulance. Butch and Ron insist they should follow, they should be by Timmy's side.

At the hospital waiting room, Butch and Ron surround Timmy's wife until they are joined by their own wives, who take up the task of comforting her. Butch and Ron anxiously wait for any news from the ER doctors and nurses. Secret Service agents are posted all around the hospital. The president phones Butch to express his concern. News channel trucks fill the streets. Bright portable lights dot the parking lot as on-scenes pass updates from the ER to their respective anchors in New York, Atlanta, Chicago, and Los Angeles. Thousands of people gather in a vigil around the hospital, as close as the police lines allow.

The waiting goes on and on. In the waiting room, people speak only in hushed voices. No one sleeps. Some of the campaign staffers keep busy by fetching coffee. Ron disappears from time to time to speak to the press in a makeshift press room in the hospital chapel. The updates on Timmy are few and infrequent.

Around 4:30 am, Butch dozes off on a sofa. He's jolted awake when the PA system announces, "Dr. Jameson, please call 214. Dr. Jameson, please call 214."

Butch gets back on his feet and walks over to Ron. "Any word? I think I might have conked out for a minute."

Ron chuckled, "I think that's all it was. About a minute." His voice changed to serious. "No. No word. They're still working on him in there." Then his voice quivered slightly. "Butch, it doesn't look good."

A few moments later a doctor in scrubs entered the room. Ron, Butch, and Meghan steered him toward Mrs. Connors. A small cordon of agents encircled them.

"As you know, Mr. Connors has suffered a massive heart attack. He's unconscious now, and we're in no rush to wake him. We've done all we can for him. His body needs time to heal before he wakes up. The next forty-eight hours are critical. All we can do is monitor his situation. I don't want to mislead you in any way. We are prepared for the worst and hope for the best. You might want to get the family together."

As the doctor turned to leave, Butch touched his shoulder. "Thanks, Doc. We appreciate everything your team is doing to help Timmy."

The doctor nodded. "Sure thing, Mr. President-Elect."

The campaign spokesperson followed the doctor out of the room but turned toward the makeshift press room.

While others gathered around Mrs. Connors, Butch stood frozen in place, not sure he heard that last bit correctly. He looked at Ron. "What did he just call me?"

Ron pulled him to the side. "A lot of things have happened tonight and are going to happen today, tomorrow, and for a while. Unless Timmy miraculously leaps out of that bed and until we hear anything to the contrary, you are indeed the president-elect. Frankly, I don't know what's going to happen. The Electoral College needs to confirm the election results before it's official. And that's not going to happen until mid-December. But we need to be prepared. And that makes you the man. Butch, you're the next president of the United States."

It took a minute for this to sink in, but when it did, Butch placed his hand on Ron's shoulder.

"Okay, listen up!" He glanced at his watch. "It's almost six. That means it's nine on the east coast. Let's make some phone calls. Talk to some people. Find out where we are constitutionally and legally. Get our ducks in a row. We need some people at campaign headquarters. Ron, pick someone to run that show. For the time being, you and I need to be here. Send someone to your home to get what you need in the way of fresh clothes and toiletries. We'll talk to the hospital to see if they have a locker room or someplace where we can get cleaned up. If we get hungry, we can either grab something at the cafeteria here or send out for food.

For the next forty-eight hours, we stay here and hope and pray that Timmy's going to wake up and get back on his feet. If the hospital can't accommodate us, we need to find someplace close by. First and foremost, we want to be here to be close to Timmy. But we still have a lot of work to do to get from here to the inauguration. We've got to be prepared. The country is depending on us!"

The small group of campaign people and family were frozen in place, hanging on Butch's every word, taking it all in.

Butch sensed they were still stunned by the events of the night as well as lack of sleep. "Well," he said. "What are you waiting for? Let's get moving! Chop chop!"

Meghan and Ron's wife placed their arms around Timmy's wife's shoulders. "Don't worry, we're all going to be there with you and Timmy for the inauguration. Ron and Butch are going to do everything they can so Timmy's there for his date with destiny."

Chapter Thirty-Three

Anyone Have a Plan?

They found a teaching hall at the hospital to accommodate everyone. About seven rows of tables were filled, subordinates taking a seat directly behind their bosses. Laptops, tablets, and pads were spread across the desks, and everyone checked their phone. The cacophony of ringtones led one of the staffers to direct everyone to switch their phones to vibrate.

Butch and Ron sat at the front of the room. Meghan was at the far side of the front row.

Ron began, "You should have received an email with an outline of the things we need to address immediately. Certain items are highlighted for each team. If we're going to make this work, we need to be prepared to work twenty-four-hour days, just as we're going to have to do after the inauguration and for the next four years. You'll sleep when you can. You'll eat when you can. When you signed up for this campaign, you signed up for the long haul."

Butch was the first to react. "What do you mean if we're going to make this work?"

"Well, you know. You actually being president of the country," Ron said.

"You know," Butch said, "despite everything that's happened these past few months, I really had no idea we'd be where we are today. I wasn't planning to call anything off then chalk it down as a great experience, though. And now that Timmy's won, that we've won, I'm all in! We're going to do what we have to do to make the Connors administration the best in the history of this country."

One of the campaign deputies whispered not too softly to the person next to him, "You really think they're going to let Butch be the next president?"

"Who's they?" Butch answered loudly, so the whole room could hear him.

"The people in Washington who actually run this country," the man answered.

Butch shook his head. "But the people. You know, we the people. The people run this country."

Meghan looked at him and said, "Oh, honey, you're the smartest man I know, but you need to watch something other than ESPN! This country is run by people who aren't going to let someone like you tell them what they should be doing. And they've been running the country for a long, long time. You're just a temporary employee."

Butch looked around the room. No one made eye contact with him.

He turned to Ron.

"You know, Butch, I'm afraid she's right. It's only a matter of time."

Butch couldn't believe his ears. "Matter of time until what?"

Meghan answered, "Until a group of congressmen and senators and justices and lawyers burst through those doors with reams of paper. Paper that says you're nothing and don't belong anywhere near the White House, except maybe as a visitor getting a tour of the old place."

Butch looked up at the ceiling for a moment and then stood up and looked at the assemblage of wannabe White House staffers. "So, we can either sit back and wait for the doors to burst open or we can make the most of this election, of Timmy's election, and take the fight to them!"

When no one said anything, he paced around the front of the room.

"You know, when I'm in the ring, the promoter tells me what he wants and how long he wants it to last. And from the second that bell rings, until my time is up, my opponent and I give it our all, because that's what the people expect of us. We've never just stood around and watched the clock, waiting for our time to run out. And I'm not about to do anything like that now!"

He slammed his fist on the lecturer's table, startling everyone. "If it's a fight they want, it's a fight they're going to get! But we're the ones who are going to call the match!"

He turned to Ron. "Get Angelo on the phone and tell him to get his butt here. We're getting the band back together and we're on a mission!"

Chapter Thirty-Four

When a Plan Comes Together

Angelo dropped everything and rushed to the hospital where Timmy was hanging on. He brought along a huge folder of eight-by-ten photos, placed it on a table, and sat down next to Butch. With a Sharpie in hand, Butch wrote yes on a piece of paper and no on another and laid them at the edge of the table.

Angelo pulled out a photo of a rough, unshaven man wearing a leather mask. The Milkman. Butch and Angelo smiled and placed the photo on the yes pile.

Ron watched from the side and picked up the photo. He shook his head and took the Sharpie and wrote the word Hell above the word No and placed the photo in that pile.

Butch glanced at Angelo and picked up the Sharpie and wrote Oh Hell above the word Yes and moved the Milkman photo back to that pile. Angelo high-fived him for that.

The wrestler and the promoter worked through the photos for a couple of hours, sorting them into the two piles. And they made it clear Ron could watch, but he didn't have a voice in the sorting. After the sorting process was over, Butch and Angelo started making phone calls. That afternoon Butch explained the task ahead for Ron. He would be staying at the hospital and keeping tabs on Timmy's recovery while Ron and Angelo would visit some wrestlers.

Ron and Angelo first visited a playground and saw a few moms and their children. Near the swings they found a six-foot-eight 380-pound man with a blue Mohawk and a dozen earrings, alternately pushing two children in their respective swings.

Hello, Charles "the Tasmanian Devil" Holmes.

When Charles saw Angelo, he ran over and picked him up with a bear hug. Angelo introduced Ron. The campaign manager hoped to avoid a bear hug, so he nervously offered his hand to the Tasmanian Devil.

Angelo said, "Charlie, we need your help. Can we talk?"

"Sure," Charlie said. "But what about my kids?"

Ron looked at a couple of accompanying staffers. "Can you help us out for a few minutes?"

The three men adjourned to a nearby bench, and Ron

and Angelo explained the plan to Charlie. There was a lot of smiling and laughing.

After Charlie signed on, Angelo and Ron visited the next person on their list.

They entered a small, dingy bookstore and made their way through the shelves of books toward a cluttered counter in the middle of the store.

The owner, a man in his forties, looked up from his book. He wore dollar store reading glasses and was dressed in tweed. Angelo introduced Earl "The Professor" Hannaway to the campaign manager.

Before Angelo could say another word, Earl lifted a finger to keep him from interrupting before he finished the paragraph he was reading. He marked his place with a makeshift bookmark and closed the book.

Earl put the book down and stood up. As he greeted Angelo with a smile and a handshake, Ron saw he was about six-foot-four and weighed around 280 pounds.

"Professor, if you've got a minute, we'd like to talk to you about something very important," Angelo said.

Earl smiles as his eyes scan the raggedy store. "Well, as you can see, I'm very busy. But for you, I'll make the time!"

The three men walked over to an open area with a mishmash of chairs, rockers, and stools.

Angelo and Ron's next meeting took some time to arrive at. The scenery changed to a snow-covered countryside. Angelo had wisely procured a four-wheel drive, because the driveway they ascended had not been cleared since the last snowfall.

The promoter detested cold weather. He dressed like an Eskimo for this meeting. Snow was still falling when he and Ron walked to the house. But when they heard the sound of someone chopping wood, they followed it to the back of the house, where they saw Harry "the Axe" Feldman.

Harry wasn't as tall as the Tasmanian Devil or the Professor, but his size was impressive. He was only six feet tall, but his chest and arms were humongous. Harry wore jeans and boots, and his flannel shirt lacked sleeves, which exposed his massive twenty-inch biceps.

When he saw his visitors, Harry thrust the axe into a piece of wood and greeted the Eskimo.

"Angelo, you old son of a gun! What brings you way out here? You want me to do a job for you?"

"You know, Harry," Angelo said, pointing to the woodpile, "They have machines to do that for you."

Harry chuckled. "Yeah, well, I trust these machines to do all my chores!" And he pointing to his arms.

"Is there someplace we can talk and not freeze to

death?" Angelo asked, noticing that Ron was visibly shivering.

"You always were a wimp about a little cold weather," the Axe teased. "I think you've gotten even softer. Tell you what, grab some of this firewood and I'll get a fire going inside."

In addition to the fire, Harry offered the two visitors some hot cocoa. Every now and then he smiled as he listened to the plan.

The next meeting took place in a small southern church with about fifty people in attendance. Their preacher was Chris "The Saint" Plumber, and he was smaller than the men Ron and Angelo had met with.

After the church service, the pastor stood at the door, shook hands and spoke with everyone as they left. After the last person had gone, Chris greeted Angelo.

"I certainly never thought I would ever see you inside a church, much less mine!"

"Hey, Saint, great to see you again! Have you got a place we can talk?"

They went to Chris's small office. Ron and Angelo took the two chairs in front of the desk, and the preacher stopped at a nearby closet. When he turned around, he wore a white mask.

"You don't need the hood, Saint. We just want to talk," Angelo said.

"Yeah, I know," Chris said. "But I feel more comfortable wearing this." He pointed towards the sanctuary. "It's out there that I feel like I have a mask on."

Ron and Angelo shared the plan with him.

Their next meeting was at a sprawling construction site. As Ron and Angelo made their way to the structure that served as offices, they saw someone and immediately realized he was in charge. After Angelo told him who he was looking for, the supervisor pointed toward a nearby area. But before letting the men walk away, the supervisor yelled for someone to get the visitors some yellow vests, hard hats, and safety glasses.

A short time later, they approached a backhoe clearing a ditch of heavy rocks. The operator paused and looked in their direction. With a single gesture he indicated he would be with them in a minute.

Bob "The Bulldozer" Bower dropped the last boulder in the pile and swung the backhoe around, dropping the bucket about two feet from Ron.

Ron froze and looked at Angelo, who was laughing uncontrollably. He slapped Ron on the shoulder as he walked toward Bob.

Bob gave Angelo a big hug. He turned to Ron and said, "We've got a whole new row of Porta-Johns over there."

"Okay, great!" Ron answered. "Thanks for the info!"

"Well, you just kinda had a look on your face like you just crapped in your pants!" Bob said laughing.

"Hey, Bob, it's really good to see you," Angelo said. "Can we find a quiet place to talk?"

Bob glanced at his watch. "Yeah, it's about break time. We can hit the roach coach, and I'll let you buy me a burrito and a soda!"

As they walked away from the backhoe, Ron asked, "roach coach?"

Angelo laughed. "Man, you've got to get out more!"

After procuring some food, the three men found a place to talk.

Ron took a bite of his burrito, and the insides spilled onto his white dress shirt. Bob and Angelo both roared with laughter.

Chapter Thirty-Five

Let's Keep it Going!

Things seemed to be coming together. Ron and Angelo still had some work to do, but their confidence grew with each successful meeting.

Meanwhile, Butch was quietly working behind the scenes with Meghan. They reached out to former Texas congressman Robert Davis, who was well known for his impeccable character and a solid record in the U.S. Congress.

Ron and Angelo entered a Cleveland car dealership. Angelo inquired at the reception area and was directed to a sales cubicle in the front room. As the two men walked toward the cubicle, Angelo said, "You're gonna love this guy. Freddie 'Moneybags' Taylor."

As they entered the office space, Freddie was putting some papers into a file drawer. He said, "I'll be right with you."

When he turned back, he said, "Now, what kind of car can Mr. Money show—" and he saw Angelo.

"Aw, heck no! You ain't buying nothing, you cheap sucker!"

Angelo reached his hand out. "Moneybags! How're you doing, brother?"

Freddie's smile reveals the gold caps on all of his front teeth. "I'm not Moneybags these days. It's Mr. Money now!"

He sat at his desk and put on a pair of dollar-sign-shaped sunglasses. "Remember these? I still got that Midas touch, baby!"

Angelo reached across the desk and took hold of Freddie's two hands, holding them out so Ron could see them. The salesman's fingers and wrists bristle with cubic zirconium jewelry. Some in the shape of dollar signs.

Freddie quickly pulled his hands back. "Hey, keep your hands off my stones! You got your own money buried in that backyard of yours. Go mess with your own!"

Angelo sat down. "I don't think I could eat that much Cracker Jacks! But enough of this. Freddie, we'd like to talk to you."

The salesman leaned back in his chair as Ron and Angelo began to lay out the plan.

Timmy was awake and improving. He was propped up

in bed with about a half dozen machines hooked up to him. He listened as Butch laid out the plan. Gathered around his bed are Meghan, Ron, and Robert Davis.

Timmy was really trying to listen. He raised his head a couple of times, but it always fell back to his pillow. Butch adjusted the bed for him.

A nurse entered and brought a smile to Timmy's face. It's not that she was particularly attractive, though she wasn't unattractive, but rather what was on the tray she was carrying. A small cup of vanilla ice cream. His afternoon treat. Fortunately, it had softened so he could easily spoon it without assistance. But after a single spoonful, he lay back and smiled while Butch continued to discuss the plan. After a while, Congressman Davis took over the conversation.

Afterward, Ron sat down with a team of aides and a half dozen current and former wrestlers at campaign headquarters. Butch and Congressman Davis joined them shortly after the meeting began.

After introducing everyone, Ron turned the meeting over to the congressman, and he did a PowerPoint presentation on how the U.S. government works, who's who, and who does what. To their credit, everyone paid attention and engaged in a genuine back-and-forth with the congressman. Butch occasionally looked around the room, making eye contact with some of the wrestlers to ensure they understood the presentation. Whenever he detected confusion, he signaled the congressman to go back over the point and engage the wrestlers.

In mid-December the Electoral College confirmed the election results, ratifying the election of Timothy P. Conners and his running mate, Anthony Vernon.

Inauguration Day was cold and snowy in Washington D.C. Butch's eyes teared as he was being sworn in by Chief Justice Harrison Williamson.

A crowd of 1.3 million spectators filled the Washington Mall, which required the installation of several JumboTrons to allow the onlookers a clear view of the ceremonies on the West Front of the Capitol.

Timmy viewed the inauguration from his hospital bed. Tears streamed down his face as he watched the swearing-in ceremony.

Chapter Thirty-Six

Introduction Please!

The Vernon administration's press secretary was Charlie Laye, a former ring announcer. He was known as the best ring announcer in the business. He had an incredible voice and a special swagger. He had done commercials and voice-over work, but he was primarily known for doing the announcing on most of the wrestling videos on the market.

He was meeting with Butch, Ron, and Congressman Davis.

"I've taken all the data you've provided me," Charlie said, "and put together a PowerPoint to introduce the new cabinet. I tried to keep it simple, like Ron requested."

Ron smiled and gave Charlie a thumbs-up.

What followed was actually boring. Safe but boring. Each of the appointees was presented in a suit and tie, clean-shaven—or at least cleaned up a bit—and trying to look sincere.

Charlie started at the bottom and worked his way up.

"Our nominee for secretary of homeland security is Mr. Andrew Holmes." In the photo, Andrew's neck was so large that he couldn't button the top button of his shirt. So, he tried to cover the gap with his tie.

"Our nominee for secretary of transportation is Mrs. Charlotte Williams."

Charlotte "School Bus" Williams is an athletic African American. She had formerly wrestled for Angelo, and later she managed other wrestlers.

Butch was not happy with the presentation. Ron was incredulous. And the congressman tried to say something positive. Charlie continued, nonetheless.

"Our nominee for secretary of defense is Mr. Kyle "The Milkman" Frazier." Kyle has long, bushy hair and a full beard with a few bald spots. He is missing a few teeth and has multiple scars on his forehead and face. Kyle isn't smiling in the photo.

After what Butch thought was too much time, Charlie intoned, "Our final nominee is Congressman Robert Davis for secretary of state."

As the only professional politician in the group, Davis actually looks the part. His suit is perfect, his hair is groomed, and he has a natural smile that fits the image.

Charlie paused and looked at everyone for their approval. Ron, however, is the only one smiling.

"Charlie," Ron said, "that was very good! I think you captured the inner essence of our nominees. What did you think, Butch?"

Butch gave the congressman a look and motioned for him to go instead.

Davis stumbled a little, trying to find the right words. "Well, you were asked to do a very complicated and important task, and I think you've done an excellent job of putting together a snapshot of the team we've assembled. Good job," he said.

Butch spoke first to the congressman. "My gosh, you're good! I'm so glad you're on my side."

Then he looked at Charlie and Ron. "Guys, I had a really different idea of how we should present the members of our cabinet. Charlie, why don't you stick around, and you and I can go over some ideas."

Ron asked, "Do you want me to stick around?"

"No, Ron. I think you've done a great job of laying the foundation. Now, I just want to put a little kick in it."

Ron took that as a compliment and left.

Butch went over his ideas with Charlie. The press secretary asked clarifying questions about what Butch was looking for in the presentation and offered some suggestions that Butch liked. They were finally on the same page.

The next day Butch assembled his cabinet and other team members in the White House Theater. He addressed the group from a podium on the stage.

"Charlie and I have spent a little time putting together a brief video to introduce each of the new cabinet members to the country. We hope you enjoy what we've put together!"

The lights dimmed and loud rock music started to shake the room.

Charlie, dressed in a tuxedo, stood center stage and held an oversized microphone.

"Welcome, America! I'm your new presidential press secretary, Charles Laye! Please join me in welcoming your new and improved cabinet!"

The first of many cabinet members made a dramatic appearance through a cloud of smoke. Earl Hannaway emerged in a long-sleeve gray workout top and matching gray yoga pants. Earl danced straight at the camera, doing several spins and splits along the way.

Charlie continued the introductions: "With a Harvard degree in something I can't even pronounce, at six feet tall and weighing 255 pounds, your new secretary of energy,

Earl "The Professor" Hannaway!"

After a moment in front of the camera, Earl peeled off and went to the far end of the stage.

"And next, from a landfill in your hometown, at six-foot-two and weighing 275 pounds, your next secretary of the interior: Robert "The Bulldozer" Bower!"

Bulldozer Bower wore jeans and work boots, a long-sleeve work shirt, and a hard hat. He walked out as if he were driving a bulldozer, doing stagger steps and moving his arms back and forth. Bob zigzagged across the stage before stopping in front of the camera.

The next cabinet member is Claudette Williams. She carried herself well, dressed in slacks and a blouse and looking foxy. The tall African American woman struts to center stage and then makes her way to the camera, snarling as she walks.

"She may be driving your children to school or teaching them to wrestle! Your new secretary of transportation is Claudette "School Bus" Williams!"

Claudette peels off as the next person enters.

"And with more than thirty years of public service, the man with the plan, the man with all the answers, the man with the great hair, your next secretary of state! Give it up for Mr. Robert Davis!"

The congressman emerges coughing from the smoke,

waving to try to clear the air in front of him. He is an impressive figure and is smiling from ear to ear.

When the video ends, the lights come up, and after a moment of silence, the small group begins to applaud. Slowly at first, then thunderously.

Butch went back onstage.

"Now that's how you introduce a cabinet! Obviously, we didn't have time to put the whole cabinet together, but over the next couple of weeks, Charlie and Ron will meet with you to schedule your filming. All of our lives are changing now. We need to watch what we do, watch when we do it, and watch who we do it with. We're all working for America now. We answer to the people who put us here. Don't screw this up! Got it?"

Chapter Thirty-Seven

Meet the Press

Charlie's daily press conferences were the most amazing performances the Washington press had ever seen. He was even surprising himself by doing something he had never done before.

Butch had just finished his daily workout. He was dressed in sweats and had a towel around his neck. As he walked by the White House briefing room, Butch decided to make a surprise visit.

Charlie was a little startled when he saw Butch enter. He excused himself and walked over to Butch. "Mr. President, this is a surprise. Can I help you?"

"Relax, Charlie. I just wanted to pop in and see what these briefings are like." He smiled and waved at the reporters.

"They don't look that tough. Let me say hello."

He started to walk to the podium, but Charlie said, "Butch, I mean, Mr. President, I wouldn't do that if I were you."

Butch just looked at him and said, "Charlie, don't sweat it! I've faced tougher crowds than this. Just gonna say hi and introduce myself to your buddies."

Butch walked up and adjusted the microphone. "Good morning!" he said. "I guess you know who I am, but I have no idea who you all are. I just wanted to pop in and say hi. While I'm here, does anyone want to ask me anything?"

The first senior reporter said, "Mr. President, Donald Pleasant. I've been covering presidents for close to twenty-five years and this is a first. I'd like to ask, what do you think qualifies you to be president?"

Butch was taken aback. "Really? Everything that's going on in the world, and that's what you want to know? Give me a break! Anyone else have something they want to ask me?"

A young reporter raised his hand. "Well, Mr. President, I don't want this to sound disrespectful, but what really qualifies you to be president?"

"Well, bud, okay. Great question! I'm glad you asked. I'll tell you what qualifies me. One, I'm a native-born citizen of the United States. Two, I'm over thirty-five years of age. And three, I've never been convicted of a felony!"

Butch walked offstage and paused in front of Charlie. He took his towel off his neck, placed it around Charlie's neck, and pulled him close. "You deserve more money for having to deal with this bunch of a-holes every day! I want you to escort these jobronies out of the White House. No sandwiches. No snacks. And collect their press badges. Next time I come out here to talk, it will be in front of people who want to know how we're going to fix the messes we have to fix. Not to ask me stupid questions!"

Charlie quickly passed the towel to one of his aides and returned to the podium. "That concludes today's press briefing. As you leave, please turn in your press badges." And then he gestured for the security officers to follow his instructions.

Chapter Thirty-Eight

There's a New Sheriff in Town

"Good evening. I'm Jan Arnold, sitting in for David Drucker. Before we get to the news, we are joining a live news conference with Senator Buford 'Skip' Buckhorn."

The senator said, in his thick southern accent, "Yes, we are taken aback by Mr. Vernon's bully tactics. I represent a hardworking Christian constituency, and I am highly offended by his characterization of myself and my fellow senators as 'lazy, bloodsucking leeches'! Why, just the other day, a lovely young lady came up to my limo and told me that some of her kinfolk were talking about inviting Mr. Vernon to a good old-fashioned lynch party and that they had a proper necktie they wanted to present him. Of course, that's completely her opinion."

The president, however, was making a difference with both his words and his actions, whether the distinguished senator knew it or not.

There was a total absence of support for the senator's views. The ensuing discussion on the news took exception to the senator's crass racism. In fact, the news channels and talk radio, as well as every element of social media, harangued Senator Buckhorn until his office issued an apology and reported that the senator had taken a short leave of absence—for health reasons.

A short time later, the presidential entourage and a gaggle of reporters visited a public elementary school in a depressed neighborhood in Compton, a large rural city south of downtown Los Angeles. The principal led them on a tour of the school, pointing out the positives and the negatives, and ticking off a list of the kinds of improvements they believed so many public schools across the country needed.

After a tour of the classrooms and labs, the group went out to the playground to watch the kinds of recreation the school sponsored for the children. Butch joined in on a game of kickball with some of the kids.

An inning or two later, Butch addressed the reporters. "This is one of the most important issues my administration is going to tackle. We're going to find a way to improve our schools, not just by throwing money at them, though there's going to be some of that, but by stressing teacher training and solid curriculums. We don't need unnecessary bureaucracies that focus on grades. We need teachers who care, who invest themselves in these children. And if we can do that with tax credits for student debt or whatever else we can do, we're going to try. We're going to look at every suggestion, consider every idea. We're going to find a way to enhance education for everyone because an educated citizen is the bedrock of this republic. And we're going to do everything we can to enhance physical education and recess. There's more to life than just studying. All children need to get off their butts and get out here and move!"

Butch noticed one of the students trying to get his attention.

"What? Okay. Looks like it's my turn. I suggest you all go way out there, because I'm getting ready to kick this ball into the next county!"

He handed his coat and tie to Meghan. Then an idea hit him.

Butch waved all the children in from the field and told them that this time they were going to watch, while the reporters and aides in his entourage took the field.

As soon as the adults were in place, Butch stepped up

to the plate. After a couple of tries, the SE1 reporter on the mound rolled the ball perfectly. The president of the United States caught it just right, sending it far out into center field. The students cheered as Butch rounded the bases, while the reporters tried to collect the ball and get it to home plate.

They were too late.

A week or so later, New York Congressman Perry Norman criticized Butch in a fund-raising speech. One of the news channels was in the area by chance and they captured the whole speech on video, showing it to the country that night.

"So, this overgrown buffoon is making a mockery of the government system that I and others have worked and sacrificed our whole lives to stabilize," the congressman said. "Why, my family and I actually had to cut short our Hawaiian fact-finding seminars in order to return to our country estate, bunker in, bring my personal staff up to speed, and start working on a way to get this Neanderthal out of office!"

The hourly news panels dissected every word of the congressman's address. For days he was pilloried by the press. On the fourth day a spokesperson for the congressman declined to comment but revealed, "For family reasons, the legislator would be on a short leave of absence."

Two weeks later the president's entourage toured an inner-city hospital in St. Paul, Minnesota, and spent a great deal of time in the children's ward. Accompanying the president were officials from the Centers for Disease Control, the Health Resources and Services Administration, and the Bureau of Primary Health Care. The press followed along as the officials were given a tour of the facility, but Butch asked them not to photograph or record them when they were visiting the children's ward. Meghan and he had gifts for every child, and for a short time the first couple read stories to the children.

Butch was sitting on the edge one of the children's beds. After he finished reading her a story, he gave the book to her, and then he gave her a hug. A photographer was getting really close to capturing the moment but he caught Butch's attention instead.

The president stood and walked over to the photographer. He held his hand out for the camera and handed him a book with his other hand.

"Now it's your turn," Butch said. "See that young boy over there?"

The photographer nodded. "Yes, Mr. President."

"Go read a story from this book to him," Butch said. "I'll hold your camera."

Butch walked over and stood by Meghan. She hugged him. A few minutes later all the press corps as well as a few Secret Service agents were sitting with a child and reading to them.

The doctors and nurses had never seen anything like it.

A month later the presidential entourage visited a low-income neighborhood in Helena, Alabama. After a tour by Housing and Urban Development officials, Butch held a press conference. He wore a hard hat in front of an abandoned house.

"Today we start our Clean Street project. We are going to bulldoze any abandoned house that is suspected of being used as a crack house. This house behind me is coming down. The debris is going to be hauled off, and the land is going to be sold to the highest bidder. All money collected from these sales will go to local rehab centers. For every crack house we tear down, I want to open a room so we can help people kick this deadly habit."

Butch turned to Bob "The Bulldozer" Bower, the secretary of the interior, with the cameras still rolling. He gave Bob a signal, and the secretary drove the bulldozer through the middle of the house. The crowd that had followed the president's group through the neighborhood voiced its approval.

A week later political analyst Pamela Manetti led a heated discussion over the initiatives forwarded by the Vernon administration.

"The legalities of this sham go far beyond numerous breaches in our Constitution. There are at least a dozen class-action lawsuits being pressed by both Democratic and Republican action interests. As we speak, all of these are on the docket of the next session of the Judicial Grand Jury. Mark my words," the analyst announced, "Mr. Vernon's days as commander in chief are going to be few!"

Then she looked into the camera. "Live it up while you can, Mr. President!"

A short time later the presidential entourage visits a church-sponsored soup kitchen. They all don aprons and dish out food to the long line of homeless and indigent souls who regularly show up for whatever food the church has to offer. Those who aren't serving food volunteer to cook, clear tables, and wash dishes.

Butch's agenda and example receive widespread acceptance across the country. Many communities report they have never seen the spirit of volunteerism to the degree that is now sweeping the country.

Chapter Thirty-Nine

Ups and Downs

While Butch and company were fully engaged with multiple initiatives, Butch regularly checked in with Timmy to fill him in on the big picture and to check on his recovery. Turns out, Timmy had some serious complications from the triple bypass surgery that saved his life. He found that physically, he was becoming a new man. There were also significant parts of the comedian's soul that had made amazing changes. Butch spent as much time with Timmy as he could, sharing life changes that he needed to make to help him physically and spiritually. Timmy even allowed Butch to pray for him when they visited together. The first time Butch prayed for Timmy, it brought tears to both of their eyes. It was amazing to see the transformation that was taking place in Timmy's life. He was still the comedian that everyone loved, but he was also becoming a man with a spiritual side.

Timmy's doctors had put him on a strict diet, which didn't go over very well with him. He had a sixty-year history of eating whatever he wanted. Fortunately, no one snuck him any cheeseburgers, fries, or shakes during visiting hours, despite his pleas. Not even a burrito. In the end, he had no option but to comply with the hospital dietician's menus.

Over time his weight dropped, and when physical therapy began, his strength and stamina improved. At the same time his spirits improved, his humor changed from confrontive to sympathetic. All the nurses came to love being around Timmy. He made them laugh and brought a lot of joy to their shifts. They looked forward to coming in every day. In the end, they had to devise ways to see which of them would be Timmy's nurse for their shift.

The doctors, on the other hand, certainly were tested when it came to dealing with Timmy. They lacked the sense of humor that the nurses had in abundance. And they especially failed to appreciate Timmy's antics, such as scrawling jokes and filling their charts with graffiti.

For a while Timmy didn't shave, and he let his hair grow out. Soon he had a full beard, and he joked about being a reject from the seventies. Then he decided he liked the look and the options he now had. He settled on pulling his hair back into a ponytail.

One day his therapist decided Timmy was ready to walk the halls, to test his stamina. A doctor on shift decided to observe the walking test for himself to see how Timmy was progressing. After all, it wasn't every day you had a patient who had been elected president of the United States in your hospital.

Timmy seemed to be doing well on the walk. Occasionally he paused and stuck his head into each room he passed. Depending on what he knew about the patient in the room, he offered encouragement or some borderline salacious humor to leave a smile in his wake. He was learning the power of suggestion and how understatements received stronger laughs than overstatements. Sometimes he encountered nurses who were a tad too rigid, too strict with their patients, and he found that his new style of slightly inappropriate comments disarmed them. They either glared at him in response or blushed at the realization that sometimes a lighter touch went a lot further in caring for patients.

At some point during the walking test, Timmy noticed a doctor who was being a little too observant. And then he staggered and fell against the wall and moaned. The doctor pulled the therapist out of the way, grabbed his arms, and yelled for a wheelchair. He couldn't say the word stat enough.

After a beat, Timmy straightened up, looked the doctor in the eye, smiled, and said, "Gotcha!"

Embarrassed, the doctor released Timmy and exited the floor as quickly as he could.

Timmy looked at the therapist. "Some guys are just a little too high strung, don't you think?"

The Washington establishment was up in arms about the President's across the board approach at leading from the front. This was not the way things were done. No one person could assess, evaluate, and determine the necessary action by the federal government. There were committees to do that. And they needed time to assess and evaluate, and then realize something had changed that required more assessment and more evaluation. Decisions required years of preparatory work. Sometimes decades. Of course, no one wanted to waste time. After all, there were needs, and people were involved. But no one accomplished anything with knee jerk reactions to a particularly deplorable problem. The American public deserved no less than responsible, reasoned action from their elected officials.

Butch Vernon had to be stopped before he could significantly change the way things got done. His actions threatened to alter the structure of a bureaucracy that had taken more than a century to build.

At the White House, Daniel Owen, the president's legal counsel, sat down with Butch and a handful of chief advisers to assess the backlash from the political establishment.

"These are the latest injunctions filed against you with various congressional committees," he said. "I'm also hearing whispers that some of the leadership have contacted select federal circuit judges to issue stays against the Clean Street project particularly."

The ensuing discussion took the rest of the afternoon and early evening.

Finally, Butch said, "Then that's it. That's what we're going to do, and frankly the sooner we do this, the better. Thank you, everyone. Go home and get some sleep. We're all going to need it."

Chapter Forty

Face the Nation

The White House scheduled a primetime slot for the president to address the American people from the Oval Office. Since this was his first such address, all the networks and news channels made the time available.

Meghan put her hand on his shoulder. "You know I'm proud of you, right?"

"You are, huh?" Butch teased.

"Yes! It takes a lot of courage to do what you're going to do," she said with a smile.

"It's just a little chat with about a hundred million people," he quipped. "No big deal."

"You know what I mean, Butch! I know what this job means to you."

"Meghan, I feel as if this is what I was born to do. I have enjoyed the challenge of this office, but someone more qualified needs to do this job now. God placed me here to do what I'm doing tonight. We're going to be fine."

Ron knocked on the door. Butch kissed Meghan. He and Ron went over some last-minute updates as they walked toward the Oval Office. Butch paused and looked around this special place before he took his chair at the resolute desk. The camera crew made some adjustments to the equipment.

Congressman Davis, Ron, and Meghan stood across from Butch, forming a small line in front the fireplace. Meghan quietly appreciated how comfortable he looked.

The White House communications director counted down the president's cue that they were live.

"Good evening, America. I would first like to report to you that Timmy Conners is doing better each day. He has received the best medical help anyone could receive. He sends his love and thanks for all your prayers and expressions of kindness to him and his family.

"It seems as if I've given a few thousand speeches over the past dozen years. Most of them were given from a wrestling ring. Most of them had the same theme: 'I don't like to lose,' 'You're gonna need an army to beat me,' 'I want to be the type of champion other people can look up to.' My address tonight has those same tones, but there will be a different result. There are some things I can do by

Executive Orders, but the majority of my suggestions tonight will have to be passed by the House and the Senate. I'm hoping that by pointing them out to you, the American people, you will hold them accountable. I think they have forgotten that they work for you, you don't work for them.

"Life is a struggle. In everything we do, we face some kind of opponent. The guy in the cubicle next to you who wants your job, the faceless traffic you fight through every day and night, bill collectors, some illness that sneaks up on you. Most of what we do in life is a battle.

"One of the biggest battles we face regularly is the daily struggle against the very people we elect to office. Lifetime fat cats who haven't lifted a finger in ages to do a lick of work, who are so far removed from real life because of the special bubble they have created to live in.

"My goal to eliminate some of your daily battles starts with making some big changes right now. But again, it will take you holding them accountable.

"Every day, Democrats blame Republicans, and Republicans blame Democrats. I would like to suggest tonight that we start by fighting not for our parties, but for the American people!

"When I was a boy, I'd ask my mom for a couple of dollars to see a movie with my friends. My mom was a single mom, and she worked two jobs. She explained to me about the debts she faced every day, and if I wanted to see a movie, I had to earn the money to do so. Well, I found some work and earned the money! I learned at an early age that if I wanted something, I'd have to work for it or go without.

"That's exactly what's happening in our nation today. We're asking Mom for a couple of dollars for something we can probably do without. And Mom tells us we're over twenty trillion dollars in debt! So, you want some money, go out and work for it or go without. The next time we send someone a check for a couple hundred dollars, it should be because they spent some time picking up trash in the community or doing something constructive to help their community.

"I'm going to talk to some politicians now, specifically senators and members of the House. Your future pay should be no more than the average enlisted soldier serving our country. Your healthcare should come through the Veterans Administration, not by-passing laws about our healthcare that don't affect you. And when you leave office, you should receive the same benefits as our military retirees.

"I want you to know the White House is posting a petition on the White House web page tonight asking Congress to enact a term limits bill before the end of the current session. I urge every registered voter in the country to sign this petition online. Why is this necessary? Because nothing will change until we have term limits. If you are elected to serve in the House or the Senate, and you leave Washington richer than you were when you entered office, you aren't serving your constituency. You're only taking care of yourself. And that makes you a corrupt politician. Let me just make it real plain. If you leave office richer than you were before you entered that office, you are a corrupt politician.

"Everyone in public service in Washington needs to remember that we serve the people of this country first. So, if you really want to serve, it will be because of the fire within you to resolve the problems this country faces and to make this country a better place in which to live. You weren't elected to line your pockets and advance your position in life.

"In addition, an emphasis needs to be placed on our children and elderly citizens. We can no longer look the other way at the abuses they are suffering at our hands. I know this isn't going to be popular, but we can no longer afford to reward unwed mothers who continue to bring children into the world and then expect us to support them. Something has got to change.

"First responders also need our attention. Today,

nearly twenty-eight percent of all first responders have to have second jobs just to make ends meet. Either these fine people have too much free time on their hands, or we aren't paying them enough. They are our life's blood, and they need our attention.

"Crime must also be addressed. We are way too soft on criminals. Again, we are paying for their mistakes. Let's let the criminals pay their own way. If you go to prison, you work. Your reward for that work will be a bed to sleep on and three homegrown meals you will help to grow and prepare. In my prison-reform proposal, I hope that we can release those who have served their time for first-time offenses.

"Recently, Congressman Robert Davis and I spent some time in Afghanistan, personally putting troops on the planes that would bring them home. It's our goal to have eighty-five percent of our troops back on American soil before the end of the year. This is especially important because the vast majority of these troops are from National Guard units that have been deployed overseas for too many tours of duty. We have far too many battles in our own backyard to risk the lives of our people on foreign battlefields, particularly when the very people we vow to protect have no interest in their own security.

"I would also like to suggest that we put soldiers on our

borders. For too long we have sent our young men and women to foreign countries to protect their borders while criminals have been allowed to cross our borders with the people attempting to repeatedly come into our country illegally. I love immigration. Our country has been built by immigrants. But we have laws that determine the right way to come into our country. Several of our large cities are overrun with crime. It's not safe to live in those cities. The liberal mayors and politicians do absolutely nothing to help with the situation. Why not put our military in those cities to help with the crime problems instead of having them police communities on foreign soil?

"Within our borders we value the right to free speech and dissent. But the First Amendment does not protect anarchists and foreign agents who are devoted to the destruction and dissolution of the United States of America. During the Vietnam War, a significant segment of the anti-war movement touted the old saying 'America, love it or leave it.' If you don't want to be here, if you don't cherish what this country stands for, if you despise the American people, that speaks loudly that you really don't want to be here. I would like to suggest that we provide a one-way ticket to whatever Godforsaken country your heart desires. We will pick you up, drive you to the airport, and wave goodbye as you leave.

"One of the biggest problems in our country is we have turned our backs on the loving God who created us. I challenge all of you to look at the history of our country. If you do, you'll find that this country was founded on Christian principles. I know we have some bad things in our past such as slavery, but that was a long time ago. Our country has done a lot to make up for the sins of the past. The biggest problem today is that the politicians and liberal media are doing everything they can to turn us against each other rather than attempt to help rectify what happened long ago in our country. We have kicked God out of our government, our schools, and the entertainment that we watch. Why are we so shocked with the horrible things that take place today? It shouldn't shock us, because we have told a loving God that He is no longer welcome. I, for one, would like to invite that loving God back to our country.

"Folks, I'm not a politician. I'm a professional athlete. To be perfectly honest with you, I got into this a little reluctantly. But after I got in, I have done everything with the American people as the top priority on my agenda every day I have served. I'm sure that while I have been making this speech, a lot of politicians were probably calling the News channels that are showing my speech and asking that somebody please pull the plug. I hope and I pray that I have fired you up to hold your politicians accountable.

"And it's with these thoughts on my mind and nothing but hope in my heart that tomorrow morning I will resign from this office. I fully endorse Robert Davis as my successor. He can be the leader this country needs, the leader this country deserves! He was my choice for vice president for good reason. He is one of the finest people I have ever met. He is one of the smartest people I have ever met. I trust him completely and you can too.

"To all of you who opened the door for Timmy Connors and me to serve you for these past several months, I thank you. I know Timmy wishes he would have had a chance to follow through on his desire to serve as president.

"In fact, I wish the Washington power structure was what it should be, but since they choose to fight me for the privilege of serving you, I believe the best thing I can do is to not participate. This country has endured too much divisiveness for too long. And I will not be a party to the ugly struggle these people have in mind, which is to thwart the good work we are supposed to be doing here in Washington for the American people. I hope you will join in the work to end the corruption that has dominated the American political scene for so long. Please give your wholehearted support to Robert Davis. Thank you so much for allowing me the supreme privilege of serving you, the American people.

"God bless you. And God bless the United States of America."

Chapter Forty-One

Free at Last!

At the beginning of this story, we saw two lives that were going in opposite directions, with different morals and goals. Who would have thought they would eventually work together?

From the Sun Dome in Tampa, Florida, packed to the rafters with cheering fans, a curtain slowly opens to reveal Butch Vernon, the world heavyweight wrestling champion and the former president of the United States. The venue reverberates with "Hail to the Chief" as he walks toward the ring amid the roar of thousands of adoring fans.

Butch points to the crowd, flexes his muscles, and gives high-fives to everyone lining the aisle. On the back of his tights are sewn the words, "MR. PREZ."

At the halfway point, Butch turns around and folds his arms across his chest as he waits for someone to emerge from the curtain. A moment later, Timmy Conners appears in a red-white-and-blue suit. Between the shoulders on his jacket is sewn a single word: Manager! Two other wrestlers appear on Timmy's flanks. They are dressed as Secret Service agents. Timmy and Butch high-five as they head toward the ring! Timmy is now not only the manager for the World Champion, but he is also the highest paid comedian in the world.

The End.

About the Authors

Chris Whaley is not your ordinary American author. Beyond the pages of his books, he's woven a tapestry of experiences as a Southern Baptist pastor, a professional wrestler in the dynamic arenas of Florida, and a man who once graced the ring as 'The Saint'. The pulsating heart of his novel, "The Masked Saint", found its way to the big screen in 2016, capturing audiences nationwide.

Mentored by the legendary Great Malenko, Chris took the wrestling world by storm in the 1980s. For a decade, he showcased his prowess in Florida and across the southeastern states, even facing off against giants like The Undertaker. Chris's wrestling saga continued in Texas, where he engaged with powerhouses like Wild West Wrestling and WCCW, and made memorable appearances on independent circuits.

Chris Whaley's life story bridges the seemingly disparate worlds of faith and wrestling, embodying the spirit of dedication and passion in all his endeavors.

Mike McClaskey hails from the vibrant backdrop of Florida—the very cradle of Florida Championship Wrestling—Mike embarked on a dynamic journey. As a young man, he leapt into the wrestling arena in 1978, even before tossing his college graduation cap. Today, while he might not be grappling in the ring, the spirit of wrestling continues to pulse through the scripts he crafts.

Not just a wrestler, Mike's multifaceted talent led him to the world of cinema. With standout roles in local films, he not only captured audiences but also secured a coveted SAG membership. Ever the storyteller, Mike transitioned his vivid imaginations onto the screen, penning screenplays, commercials, and evocative short stories.

In his creative odyssey, Mike found a collaborator in Chris. Their combined genius has birthed numerous projects, with 'Mr. President?' being just one of their many masterpieces. Rest assured; the world can eagerly await more captivating tales from this dynamic duo.

https://mrpresidentbook.com/

Scan the QR code to check out more books by Chris Whaley. Or visit https://www.amazon.com/stores/author/B017RFZ72G

www.ingramcontent.com/pod-product-compliance
Lightning Source LLC
Chambersburg PA
CBHW061149120626
46546CB00005B/1990